WORK HARD-LY

Monica Iyengar pursued a bachelor's in mathematics for no particular reason. She went on to get an MBA to make a quick buck. She spent thirteen years in business and sales management, getting cheap thrills out of her designation and salary package. As a visiting faculty for organization development at M.S. University, she bursts the bubble of wide-eyed MBA aspirants. She is also pursuing a doctorate in management because a good prefix never hurt anyone.

She speaks four languages and loves the outdoors. She enjoys leading a healthy lifestyle and doesn't drink alcohol because it is not available in her dry home state. She has a husband and a six-year-old son, who need to stop rolling their eyes in the background.

You can find her on Instagram @ monica_iy

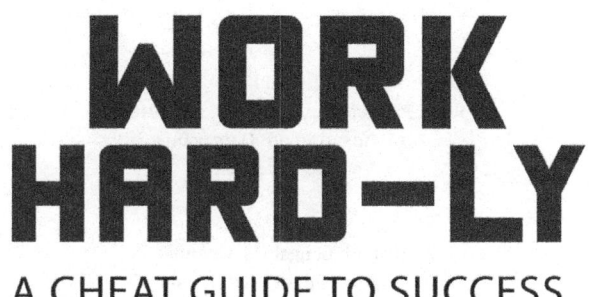

WORK HARD-LY
A CHEAT GUIDE TO SUCCESS

MONICA IYENGAR

RUPA

Published by
Rupa Publications India Pvt. Ltd 2019
7/16, Ansari Road, Daryaganj
New Delhi 110002

Sales Centres:
Allahabad Bengaluru Chennai
Hyderabad Jaipur Kathmandu
Kolkata Mumbai

Copyright © Monica Iyengar 2019

The views and opinions expressed in this book are the author's own and the facts are as reported by her which have been verified to the extent possible, and the publishers are not in any way liable for the same. Names of some people have been changed to protect their privacy.

All rights reserved.
No part of this publication may be reproduced, transmitted, or stored in a retrieval system, in any form or by any means, electronic, mechanical, photocopying, recording or otherwise, without the prior permission of the publisher.

ISBN: 978-93-5333-773-5

First impression 2019

10 9 8 7 6 5 4 3 2 1

The moral right of the author has been asserted.

Printed at HT Media Ltd, Gr. Noida

This book is sold subject to the condition that it shall not, by way of trade or otherwise, be lent, resold, hired out, or otherwise circulated, without the publisher's prior consent, in any form of binding or cover other than that in which it is published.

*For my friend and companion of
twenty years, Devang*

If you take my advice to heart,
Don't blame me if it falls apart;
If it reminds you of someone,
Doesn't mean I can't have fun;
I am only just like you,
Trying to make a buck or two;
If you choose to hold me accountable,
Be forewarned I am not responsible;
Just enjoy this ride with me,
Don't ruin it with propriety;
Consider this my formal disclaimer,
Should you fall in love with my humour.

Contents

Preface / ix

1. Introduction to Middle Management / 1

2. The Art of Being Crafty / 16

3. Team Dynamics / 22

4. Emails: Read, Write and Interpret Like a Pro / 32

5. Leadership / 41

6. How to Use Emotions Even If You Are Not a Woman? / 50

7. The Art of Delivering Presentations / 58

8. What Are Organizations Built On? / 63

9. Meetings: An Evergreen Tool / 74

10. Politics: When It's Fun for Everyone / 82

11. Women in the Workplace / 88

12. Performance Appraisal: Judgement Day / 100

13. Temporary Redemption / 106

Epilogue / 109

Preface

If you find yourself being unnecessarily worried about things that don't matter and if you feel your job has become the most unrewarding experience of your entire adult life, then you have come to the right place. Workplace worries are such nasty, stalker-like figures that follow you all the time and try to spoil all the important (read: fun) experiences of your life. And sadly, all of these worries together bring about substantial subtractions of joy from your mundane little life. Most of these fears and worries are seldom rooted in reality; hence, the whole exercise of being apprehensive about work becomes a sacrilegious waste of time.

This unease emerges from not being able to gauge what is actually important in a workplace. It is not productivity; it's not efficiency and it is definitely not competence. A lot of people find themselves stuck in jobs they don't like, with colleagues who seem insanely stupid and it comes as a surprise that they have survived adulthood. What is more saddening is that most of these insanely stupid people are doing much better than you; they are happily thriving! One may argue that obliviousness is the refuge of the happy, but that's just an ungraceful way of thinking.

So, what are the tools that you can use to make your workplace bearable, continue your job without resigning too often and still have a happy disposition? This book tries to answer these questions with the most objective outlook. It makes an attempt to help the reader gauge the situation clearly without any prejudice and find workable solutions to every problem. What makes it even more exciting is that it is equipped with real-world examples, some of which are my personal experiences. However, these implementable processes are from the worldview of a woman who spent twelve years in sales, surrounded primarily by men. So, you might find traces of feminism, but I have tried to keep it to a minimum so that it doesn't seem too unsavoury to you, dear reader.

For the purpose of this book, most leadership positions are referred to as being male. It's more fun that way. And it's also the truth.

CHAPTER 1

Introduction to Middle Management

When any new employee joins the workforce, he wants to make his presence felt; there is a deep urge to do good work and be recognized for it. The employee runs around in a frilly red dress (metaphorically speaking), just to be noticed. However, in due course, the employee grows tired, because no one cares about the expensive new red dress. He cleans this dress, looks after it and wears it diligently only to get disillusioned by its worthlessness. This employee is unable to fathom why the red dress representative of his efficiency, hard work and multitasking abilities did not have the desired effect. And this is a question that bothers many managers who find themselves on the cusp of middle management. Instead of doing things that really matter in the workplace, novice managers try and do real work which is, in my opinion, quite unnecessary. There are many interesting substitutes to real work that you will discover as you read further.

AVENUES TO STAY BUSY AND BE RELEVANT

The most important word that should find permanence in your life is 'appear'. We do so much for appearance, don't we? We buy bigger cars and houses, expensive clothes and shoes and undertake many fruitless endeavours for the sake of appearance. So, why not at the office? It is also a marketplace where only the best can thrive and rise. The rest will survive, just like you do, but it's not fun at all. The most intriguing question most managers grapple with is, 'Why do I not have enough work?' I argue most vehemently that the question you should ask yourself is, 'How can I appear busy?' Look, you want more work? All you need to do is find it. But why engage in an absolutely futile exercise when there are more gratifying ways to pass time?

Consider the following options and tell me how you feel about them.

Smoking

Smoking can be a real godsend at the workplace. As a non-smoking woman, I never had the privilege of being invited to these elitist masculine congregations.

- If you are a smoker, you automatically start getting viewed as a real man by some of your lesser mortal co-workers. You can use this to your advantage by actively joining their smoking group.
- You should make it a point to discuss how you have survived the most difficult situations on just a pack of cigarettes and a cup of coffee.
- While saying the above, make it a point to hold the cigarette between the index and middle finger and eject the smoke with your head held high. I assure you that your machismo will never be in question again and you will be looked upon as an aggressive go-getter, who never takes 'no' for an answer.
- You can make new friends by lighting a cigarette, sharing matchsticks, drowning in each other's smoke, discussing

how stupid the company's policies are and how the stipulated targets are unachievable and without any logic.
- Invest in an extravagant lighter and you will reap rich dividends. Every time you take it out in your trademark style, a lot of women will be fantasizing about you. It may not necessarily help you get promoted, but who cares.
- If you are found smoking around a woman, you can always apologize in a manly fashion and protect her from the poisonous smoke that only your superhuman lungs can endure.
- If you are not a smoker, then I am truly sorry.

P.S. An example of a lady smoker just does not work because she will not be perceived as an aggressive go-getter but rather as 'easy'; because men and women are governed by different social perception laws created by...guess who?

Laptop

If you have been bestowed with this gift, then you must endeavour to understand its non-traditional uses. A laptop can make you look perennially busy, even if you are doing just about nothing.

- You can always look seriously into the screen and pretend not to hear any questions (whose answers may not be known to you anyway), since your mind is so occupied with the next level of Angry Birds.
- When you are really workless, you can hide behind the laptop and take a quick power nap.
- Log on to Iamsobored.com and check out celebrity gossip and tell your boss that you are reviewing a competitor.
- Let's assume that you have some pests around. In that case, please open an Excel sheet, type some arbitrary

numbers and make rows and columns. Keep uttering the words 'Oh!' 'Shit' or 'Damn it!' You will appear like a mathematician trying to solve a complex problem.
- Checking some old emails or forwards may also be a good idea to pass time.
- Keep some pictures or videos handy to serve as a refreshing getaway. Always watch videos with the earphone on—as if you are in a conference call.
- In case of a power cut, your laptop should be checked for preventive maintenance and you can turn it around, remove the adaptor or engage yourself with some meaningless technical paraphernalia that may look important.

Interacting with co-workers

One might argue that talking to windbags (co-workers) is a drain on the nervous system.

But it's much better than work and it adds to your repertoire of ostensible skills. Gliding around in the confines of your workplace making small talk is serious business, not one to be taken lightly.

- Interact with some of your colleagues and discuss the latest political happenings, celebrity faux pas or travel destinations. By doing this, you are displaying how well informed you are about things other than (read: except) work. You will start getting recognized as a man of the world who knows something about everything. Putting half-baked knowledge to good use is the mark of a talented man.
- Talk dirty with some of the more masculine colleagues, to gain their macho support. A foul mouth is more popular

than you think.
- Lend an ear to the womenfolk and talk about how your wife or mother is a superwoman—someone who manages everything. This will shut the feminists up at the workplace and you may also get a stray lay on the side.
- Ensure participation in all weekend and party planning group activities. This will keep you away from work and you can be occupied doing something really meaningful. It will also help you earn some brownie points with the Human Resources (HR) department as well.

The cafeteria

Be an occasional visitor to this place because you are a busy man with tons of work on your able shoulders. But whenever you do pay a visit, keep them asking for more.

- Ensure that you taste a bit of something from everybody's lunch box. If it's a home-cooked meal, please go all out to appreciate the cook.
- Mostly, it's the support staff and people with lesser work than you who hang around in the cafeteria. Making small talk with the support staff and sharing a meal with them will prove that you are someone who does not believe in the unspoken class system that exists in workplaces.
- You must pick up a cup of coffee to keep you going for the rest of the day. On your way out, light a smoke. Slam dunk!

Hold meetings

If you are bored out of your wits and have done everything mentioned above and still have ample time on your hands, then meetings are the way to go. But before holding a meeting, you need a topic. This could be an array of subjects, such as targets, non-performance, plan of action, what to do, what not to do, how to do it, when to do it, and so on and so forth. Suppose you decide that non-performance and target achievement will be your subjects for the day. In fact, these are all-weather topics and can be used at any time—just like a face tissue.

- Call all of your subordinates ('co-workers' as a word doesn't do justice) at around say 5 in the evening, so that you can finish off everything by 6 or 6.30 and go home to a cold beer.
- Inform the subordinates about the agenda of the meeting. Ask them to get back to you with strategies to improve their performance, which is, in all likelihood, not as per expectation.
- While they are speaking, you can sit comfortably and sip a cup of tea. Think about that one hot night you spent on the beach and how you would totally love doing it all over again with that accountant woman.
- Just ensure to regularly butt in with questions or remarks such as, 'How?' 'Are you sure?' 'Can you please repeat that?' 'Good job!' 'I will be expecting better performance from now on', 'Give me the data', and so on. This will give the impression that you are listening and also keep your subordinates on their toes.
- Sometimes, you must also nod your head to imply 'agreement' or 'disagreement' because locomotion is a sign of the living.
- Please add well-thought-out comments such as, 'Good job, team', 'I want you jokers to pull up your socks' or 'Please make a presentation of what "we" discussed and

send it to me before you go home'.
- The next day can be spent collating those presentations and forwarding them to your supervisor and he is sure to be impressed with your work ethics.

You can trust your team to spin a yarn about the meeting to their neighbours in the cubicle and the legend of your tough spirit will spread like weeds. This will give you a reputation of being a taskmaster and your peers will be wary of you. You can go home and relax because you are on your way to becoming a worthy contender for senior management.

Eating out

Every once in a while, it is important to hold business meetings at some nice little romantic place where they serve gourmet meals. It can add meaning to your work life in many ways.

- It will give you a good ambience to start discussions and even if things don't go well, you can always be happy you visited the place.
- You can always claim the bills as business-meeting expenses. It doesn't really matter who you meet as long as the food is good and you can be occupied for two hours and not answer any annoying phone calls from customers or co-workers.
- You can come back late to the office and say that you were tied up in an 'important meeting' with a client, even if you were with your girlfriend.
- Business meetings can be clubbed with a long drive, especially if it is raining, and you can claim you got stuck in bad weather. That happens all the time!

Strategize

When you are devoid of any ideas and your mind has turned blank, 'strategizing' can be used quite effectively. The dictionary explains that a heraldic representation of a unicorn has a twisted horn, a deer's feet, a goat's beard and a lion's tail. This is an accurate analogy for a 'strategy' where many real things come together to create a mythical being.

Get into the meeting room either with someone or by yourself with a cup of coffee and some peanuts, and get on with it.

- You can tear some pieces of paper after scribbling on them and claim that you were 'brainstorming'.
- You can get more peanuts to energize your brains.
- You can tell everybody not to disturb you, while you take some alone time with your pet unicorn. This would be a good tool if your boss is in the office and sitting late. By engaging in strategizing, you can very deftly cover up for your lack of work and still appear busy.
- You can also involve some like-minded colleagues in this activity and make your boss feel that you are a leader in the true sense of the term.
- You can look outside the window with the disposition of a far-sighted sage and say 'This can be done' or 'We should try this' or 'I want more of this', even if you are only referring to the peanuts.

Mobile phone

No human being has been as busy as he has after the advent of the mobile phone. It has helped us become stellar examples of multitaskers. There are so many admirable cases of people texting and driving—and not dying. Whenever one is using public transport or is in a place where a lot of people are in close proximity, they choose to keep their eyes glued to a phone. They read something or frantically type or watch a video with earphones on. This has become such a phenomenon that one would feel silly sitting on a bench and just looking around. People would wonder, 'Why isn't he doing something? Why is he just being? He must be a creep.'

The best part about a mobile phone is that you can pretend to be talking to a client or a vendor even if no one else is on the other side. You can excuse yourself from wherever you are and park your bottom in a secluded room for business confidentiality.

If you are on a phone, you can claim to be doing so many things, such as sending an email, replying to client queries, negotiating with customers, reviewing competition, reading a process document or creating a process document (tough, but possible). It is better than sitting around staring at the damp spots on the ceiling.

Frantic Typing

This is when people type on a phone with urgency—as if the future of the universe depends on their reply. It can be considered a productive activity in the workplace because it's better than keeping both your hands hanging. This can be used as a clever manoeuvre if you are stuck with an annoying colleague or your boss in an elevator. It is an excellent method to avoid eye contact with co-workers/pests.

Social media

It becomes important to have a social media profile to prove that you have an active and engaging life, even if you don't. It helps you create a life that you hope to have. There's Facebook,

Instagram, Twitter, Snapchat and what was that dating thing... oh yes, Tinder. You can be busy your entire life with these social media apps and please feel free to use them at the workplace to keep yourself gainfully occupied.

Time for an anecdote:

There was a time in my work life, when a colleague whose cultural values were different from mine had sent me a Facebook Friend Request. I chose not to accept it. He was very hurt by the gesture and confronted me at the office. I told him that it was not a reflection of how I felt, that I just chose to keep my personal and professional lives separate. But he sulked and sulked and became monosyllabic in his conversations with me, so I was obligated to accept his request eventually. My ordeal was far from over because a few days later, he called me to share his apprehension about my uninhibited choice of clothing in one of my photos he found on Facebook. I banged my head for a while until Privacy Settings came to my rescue.

CONFERENCE CALLS: THE BEST TOOL TO PASS TIME

My heart bursts into a thousand rose petals when I think about the elegance of a conference call. You will be determined as a hard worker, a brilliant strategist and motivator if you invest in routine conference calls.

Don't be put off or fearful of a big word like 'conference call'. It's not the technology that's tricky; rather, it's going to be you, my crafty little bugger.

A conference call is nothing but a bunch of people talking on a phone or a speaker-like device. No biggie. But the process of booking such a call, getting the conference ID and emailing it to the participants can take up at least half a day, and that, my friend, is a well-spent half day.

You can appear busy, stressed and involved just by logging into a 'concall' (that's what smart people call it). Most people would leave you alone, consider the activity very important and give you the alone time that you deserve. This means you will not be tasked with any other work as long as you are on this call. After the call, you can claim that you are suffering from post-traumatic stress and then continue doing nothing. If you are a participant on this call, you will get about ten minutes to speak, during which you can claim poor connectivity and ask the questioner to repeat his question and in this way, time passes. Once your turn is over, you can just relax, maybe have a few biscuits, order some ice tea and listen to your colleagues getting hammered. Not a bad way to spend an afternoon appearing productive.

If you have a team, you may even consider initiating a conference call with them. It's a bit more work than being a passive participant because you will have to ask some questions, have some veiled threats and obvious criticisms handy so that you can keep throwing them around at the team members.

Conference call humiliation: How to do it

It can be the single most emotionally gratifying experience of your adult work life. It can be exciting; it can even be thrilling if there's a live video feed where you can comprehend the facial expressions of the humiliated. If a supervisor wants excellent productivity from his people, this is the way to go. People are so afraid of being on such a call, where their self-respect will be frayed vigorously in public, that some amount of post-humiliation performance can be expected.

What kind of language is passable in a conference call?

Any kind. Use abusive words generously. If there is a woman on the call, just take her name and keep apologizing. It has worked in the past and it will work for you too. Some commonly used words are 'laggard', 'slow', 'non-energetic', 'dimwit', 'pathetic', 'idiotic' and 'disgusting' to address those who don't perform as per expectation.

The whole idea of such a call is to shame individuals into performing better, because that's the best way to treat grown men and women. Fear is a great motivator and when you perpetuate it, you will realize its strength and reach.

Let me have the honour of introducing you to some one-liners that can be injected into a conference call for best results.

- Are you serious? Are you bloody serious?

There is no answer to this question. If he says, 'Yes, sir, I am,' then you can say, 'It doesn't seem so.' And you can go around in circles.

- Your level of motivation is really demotivating.

The response to this is always 'No, sir. I will try to do better.'

- You need to recharge your batteries or throw them away.

People will always say, 'Sir, you are right. I am going to charge myself all the way.' Even though in his mind he is fantasizing about electrocuting you.

- I want to hear your revised commitments. Now! Is that all?

This scares the hell out of people. They will mumble any bizarre number out of fear and then you can hold them to it and fire the hell out of them next time.

- Why don't you get up in the morning and exercise to lose all the fat in your brains?

Nobody is going to say, 'First you, then I.' People generally keep quiet because there is no reasonable response to this.

▸▸ You will be stuck in middle management forever, you dumb nut.

Nobody is going to say, 'And you are going to be with me, you jackass!' People will always say, 'I will try to do better, please give me another chance.'

▸▸ I am so tired of you. So tired.

I don't think anyone would say, 'Likewise.' It's not in the general vocabulary of subordinates.

▸▸ You have nothing more to offer. I think you are done.

'What have you offered in so much time apart from bullshit?' Any man who wants his job will not utter such a statement. You are safe.

▸▸ Even though I can't see you, I know you haven't shaved. Why?

Everyone knows that you are no superhuman. But subordinates are going to lie just to be in your good books. They are going to say, 'No, sir, it's not like that,' and then you can say, 'What do you mean by "it's not like that"?' The employee will then be just quiet because there is no dignified response.

▸▸ You have decided that you just don't want to perform. There is no way I can motivate you.

When you wish to take zero accountability for an employee's performance, this is the way to go. It's another thing that you don't know what the problem is.

▸▸ How long do I have to put up with your incompetence?

Nobody will dare say, 'As long as I have to put up with yours.' They will probably say, 'I will try better next time,' or some such unaccountable statement. So, you still have the upper hand.

▸▸ There's a limit to my patience. You have chosen to be an infantile nincompoop.

He lost you at 'patience'. Your choice of words has proved that you are more knowledgeable than the listener. Hence you win.

What to do if you are the humiliated party?

Ever heard of '*Karna ka Kavach*'? In the Mahabharata, there was a character named Karna, who had been given an impenetrable armour by a god. You need to find that armour and wear it; it's available on Amazon, like everything else.

Now, let's say you have tried everything and still find yourself plush with time.

That brings us to our next topic.

SOPHISTICATED BULLCRAP

Organizations are built by people. People often get bored, lose steam, want to do other things, get bored, want to do other things, get crazy bored. As a consequence, they have created a mechanism to engage people in mind-numbing activities in the garb of employee-engagement programmes. These programmes are sophisticated versions of activities you once did in school. It's sophisticated because this bullcrap has been designed by adults who were nostalgic about their childhood and could not find any other outlet to express this nostalgia. However, employee-engagement programmes can be effective outlets for making the most of your time at the workplace. They are easy and simple ways to keep oneself occupied.

Allow me to share a couple of examples to take you through this sustained effort of originality.

There are many sports engagement programmes where employees usually play cricket with each other. A working Saturday or Friday second half is a good time to get into something like this. Some smart alecs try to organize this on a Sunday and they should be taught a lesson.

Birthdays of employees are often celebrated in the office with cake and streamers. You should actively be a part of the organizing committee because someone is born every day. It really doesn't matter if you are not in the HR department; one can always lend a helping hand to fellow passengers.

Organizations often celebrate a 'traditional day' where employees are free to arrive at the workplace in traditional attire. You must choose an ensemble that constricts movement and has a large headgear to go with it. If you cannot move much, it will be difficult to get into meetings or engage with clients.

If your organization engages in corporate social responsibility (CSR) activities, they will be actively looking for some volunteers. Show some initiative for a change and volunteer to be a volunteer because it can fill some space on your resume and nobody can blame you for not being at your desk.

Remember, you are your principal charitable cause.

CHAPTER 2

The Art of Being Crafty

This is a tool that only winners can use. If you are not a winner, you cannot use this tool. Hence, it becomes imperative to determine whether you are a winner or not.

Take the test below and find out.

1. Are you consistently saying 'yes' to everything your boss says?
2. Do you appreciate your boss all the time for nothing?
3. Do you get tea/coffee/beverages for your boss often?
4. Do you take the laundry out for your boss?
5. Do you make yourself handy when your boss needs a lift back home or loses his car keys or needs to fill gas in his car?
6. Have you ever thought of grocery shopping for your boss?
7. Have you gone house-hunting for your boss?
8. Have you got tickets for social engagements for your boss?

If you have answered 'yes' to three or more of the above, then you truly are a winner. Once this is established, you can move on to the art of being crafty.

I do not want to label this craft as sycophancy and have a

reductionist attitude. This craft has existed since the time of kings and queens and it is so much more. This has been perfected, polished and refined to a considerable extent and there are many subtle ways of doing it. It may not be easy to learn this all at once, but 'one thing at a time and that done well is a very good rule as many can tell'.

This can be done in three different time zones: personal time, public time and shared time.

PERSONAL TIME

You need to find a way to get some alone time with your supervisor to plan or discuss a previously discussed plan or raise a simple query. When you begin to discuss the plan, he will surely jump in to show his prowess. You should pounce at this opportunity and tell him, 'Sir, I really don't know how you have such remarkable insights into things. I really want to learn to be like you.' This comment sounds sincere, though it's rehearsed. It can be used at any time for anything.

Remember, however smart your boss is, he is, after all, only human. And subtle flattery always seems heartfelt. Never use extremes when praising someone, it just doesn't sound genuine.

You can push this further at an opportune time and probe him by asking questions such as, 'How did you reach this enviable position?' or 'Give me some key pointers on how I can be as successful as you,' or 'Yours is the kind of success I want.'

These statements establish two facts: i) You like him; ii) You want to be like him. Except these aren't facts, they are your craft. He won't know what hit him and he will be quite malleable the next time you negotiate your performance or the lack of it.

PUBLIC TIME

This entails those periods of time when your boss is addressing a group of people in your presence. At this time, it would be pertinent to note that to make your presence felt, you need to grunt often or firmly say 'right' or 'yes' for every assertion asked for by your boss. You can also make it a point to ask some self-explanatory questions that may be easy for him to tackle. You should also ask questions that make him appear smarter. Don't think too much and tire yourself out; let me do all the hard thinking.

Here are some pointers: 'Sir, we should really try to achieve our targets, shouldn't we?' Or, 'Your Highness, we can move ahead with the strategy you had discussed earlier, right?'

Now, your boss is not going to say, 'Which strategy, you moron?' in public, for fear of appearing dumb. So, in all likelihood, he would say, 'Exactly, that's what I meant.'

'Boss, last time you had given an idea that really worked. Should we follow the same this time?'

An idea that worked! No man, not even the most stupid one, is going to not stake claim on this one. He will be thrilled you remembered a non-existent fact and talk at length about it. But you will have to make something up about the idea that never existed. And try to make it a *nebulous* idea, a thing that can be molded in any way by the boss.

Let's assume there is a renegade team member who has just received an offer from another company and who doesn't care any more. If he refutes your supervisor's inane statements or tries to act as if he's a free bird, cut him to size, make him shut up. (Both of you can have a pre-decided agreement on this verbal exchange as well.) This can work remarkably well for you.

Conclusively, a few helpful things happened.

First, there was at least one person in the audience who seemed to be attentive. Second, a covert appreciation of his idea happened. Third, there was a supportive audience member who tackled a rebel irritant. And you, my friend, will be remembered for these contributions for a long, long, time.

('Nebulous' synonyms: vague, unclear.
Just trying to be helpful, dear reader, not judging you).
Examples of nebulous ideas:
'I want something.'
'I really want to do something with my life.'
'I want to just fly.'
'Let's get married right now.'
'Let's have five kids for a change.'
'My wife is wrong.'
These are not stupid, they are vague because the listener can turn the discussion any way he wants to. The responses can be varied and nobody really knows what these things mean.

Especially the last one; try it sometime and let me know what happens.

SHARED TIME

Occasionally, your boss spends his precious time talking to fellow workers or doling out free advice. Don't ask me why people give advice. I read somewhere that 'Advice is like kissing; it's a pleasant thing to do and it costs nothing.' That's a reasonable clarification.

You should take this rare opportunity of telling the listeners how your boss's advice really enhanced your life and how you see new meaning in circumstances now. Like how he had asked you to effectively use your leisure time and you had nudged that old lady out of the way in a crowded marketplace. The fact that you got slapped can be omitted.

The idea is to be available whenever an opportunity to speak good untruths about your boss comes up. You must never think in terms of whether it is true or false; it's never that binary when it comes to giving compliments. It's just a reflection of how you felt after listening to his advice, and a feeling is a vast expanse of subjective, non-measurable variables. Unless you are a statistics junkie, which you are mostly not!

A REGULAR SCHADENFREUDE: REGSCHA

Pleasure derived by someone from another's misfortune is a noun that can be referred to as 'schadenfreude'. I knew I had to clarify this first because you were fumbling, my little friend. If you are a person who savours this feeling and you actively look for it, then you, my friend, are a regular schadenfreude. I just made that up.

I am not saying there is something wrong with this; in fact, scheming is better than nothing. If you are a regular Schadenfreude or *RegScha*, then you are talented, because you will energetically seek to create conditions of misfortune for your colleagues through your devious ways and that will work in your favour. You will enjoy eliminating competition through deceitful plans and that will be so much fun for you. Performance will become secondary because only you will be there.

Needless to say, nobody has to know it was you.

P.S. If Jennifer Lopez can be J.Lo, what's the problem with *RegScha?*

PET: PERSON OF EXCEPTIONAL TALENT

A PET is a trickster-vixen who can manipulate any situation to his own advantage and this manipulation will seem ordained by destiny. A PET is exceptional because he has the ability to get himself adopted and be blessed by a god in the organization. An organizational god is a person of high influence, power and a very large annual package. This could be a state god, a city god, a vertical head god or the god of gods. As a consequence of this blessing, the PET develops a halo, which makes him pretty much invincible. This halo shines brightly and blinds others with its light.

A PET has tentacles with embedded microphones at the tip, so he has access to information outside his job role. He stays ahead of the news cycle with information such as, who is getting fired, who got screwed in the performance review, who is about to offer his resignation and who got embroiled in some ethics issue.

This information will be used effectively to defer a task or ask for another responsibility or blackmail someone respectfully and professionally. The PET gathers relevant information and carries them back to the gods which, in turn, increases his god magnetism.

However, to be a PET, you need to be born with fangs and tentacles. In case you are, please write to me on my email address. I am waiting with bated breath.

CHAPTER 3

Team Dynamics

Getting along with fellow humans is an activity that has challenged the most capable amongst us. Hence I am sure it is an exercise that you, my simpleton friend, find very exhausting as well. There are a couple of situations we will discuss here. Let's begin with a situation where you are in a position to select a team.

HOW TO PICK A TEAM

Your team should be like an investment portfolio: diversified.

▶▶ Choose a person who is good at Microsoft Office suite. This is the most important person. He should be a person who has no social or personal life, preferably someone from out of town. He who thinks spending time in the office is fun. He who comes to the office on weekends for a 'break.' He should worship you like a god; you should be able to subjugate him to the maximum possible extent. You should also train him to send emails on your dictation. His competence will eliminate your reason to go to the office. You can just be.

▶▶ Choose a war horse.

Find an employee who has been in the system long enough, to know all the process loopholes. Someone who knows what to do in case a reimbursement gets stuck. Someone who can find the correct bills or rather source them for tax-saving claims. Such a person can keep you ahead in the grade curve, because you will be faster in getting things done, things that matter, such as money.

▶▶ Choose a worker bee.

A scapegoat is a must for the drudgery; one who carries your burden, one who runs for the team, one who is pliable enough to take on more. Find a person who is a natural-born worker, in whose veins the blood of hard work runs fast and thick. A worker bee works for the queen; he will die for one. The queen being you, in this case. Your wish is his command; day or night he will be at your beck and call, your 2-a.m. slave. Tell me, wouldn't you want a man Friday?

▶▶ Free average Joes.

Let's face it—some mediocre, average team members will be gifted to you either as a consequence of favours or legacy or sheer bad luck. And you need the average Joe because if everyone is smarter than you, there will be no you. Mediocrity makes space for survival, mediocrity keeps the flame burning, but barely; mediocrity makes you look good. So why not make room for it?

Phew! That was a load of work. Once you set a team in place, you need to understand how to task them to get maximum productivity.

HOW TO MANAGE YOUR TEAM (SUBORDINATES)

These are progressive times, so all those dimwits who report to you have to be called your co-workers.

Now, remember the 3Ps of being a boss:

1. You have the power to sack them;

2. You have the power to humiliate them;
3. You have the power to screw their happiness.

While you may like to consider your subordinates as an important asset, they will often surprise you by being a liability. Fear is an excellent motivator and should be used extensively to enhance control and performance. The 3Ps are not to be taken lightly; they are the absolute truth and have excellent success rates, albeit short-lived.

How to earn the respect of your subordinates?

There are two strategies you can use, depending on your proclivity. One is a short-term strategy called the Sadistic Method and the second is a long-term strategy called the Machiavellian Method.

The Sadistic Method

1. Treat them like crap
Understand that your team is a handful of jokers trying to while their time away at your expense. Hold meetings every single day, maybe even twice a day. There should be only one theme at these meetings—how pathetic these guys are. Single out individuals, berate their personalities, show them how incompetent and unemployable they are outside of your office. Once you make this a habit and create an atmosphere of incompetence, they will realize that you are the only one with a heart of gold who will take care of them. Once this hypnotherapy is completed, they will do as you say and you will now have a team of slaves under your command.

2. Never let them have fun
If they have fun, you won't, so the choice is yours to make. I suggest you burden them with your personal work. The ones

who have an attitude issue with this should be asked to shop for your groceries with *their* salary. This should be done with strict adherence to timelines because errands should be done professionally as well; it is only right. Always say no to long holidays and early check out from the office. Tell me, why do you need to say yes?

3. Hold their salary

In most companies, this may not be possible since HR may act funny when you propose to do this. In my opinion, this would be the most fruitful initiative that can ever be undertaken. Once you hold their salary, they would not only look upon you as their supreme commander but also remember never to be on your wrong side. Once they understand that the money is under your control, they are your little puppets.

The Machiavellian Method

1. Be a decepti-con artist

Sometimes, having a common enemy does wonders for friendship. Your boss can be the common enemy labelled as an unkind, unworthy, merciless little twerp. You can use this label to project yourself as a subject of undue torture. A pitiable but large-hearted creature who uses himself as a shield to protect his team. Your team will be grateful for this protection from the so-called twerp and will lay their lives on the line to uphold your honour.

Contrastingly, when you meet your boss, exhibit superlative frustration with the low capability of your team. Ensure to repeat on multiple occasions the unworthiness of your team members; this would also help keep your job safe in case of non-performance. The constant complaining will create prejudice in the mind of your boss and he would be pretty harsh the next time he meets your team. Consequently, it will bolster your team's faith in you and reinforce the earlier story about the merciless twerp.

2. Create rivalry through suffocating attention

When a parent is partial to one child, it increases competitiveness and jealously among siblings. This is something we can agree on. In the workplace, the only difference is that you have to make every team member feel as if they are the most important child. As a consequence of your suffocating attention, the subordinates may be induced to spill the beans on their colleagues or bad-mouth them and this information can be deftly used to create competitive malevolence. As they fight amongst themselves for your consideration—either through good performance or heart-rending sycophancy or both—you can pat yourself on the back for a job well done.

3. Involve the spouse

This is a strategic idea that can give you absolute control over the jerk you call your subordinate. Call all those spouses that are female, ignore the rest. Hopefully, you have only men in your team. Inform the spouses of all the ongoing employee contests in the organization. A pliable colleague from the HR department can be coaxed to share the contact details. You can promise to participate in some HR activity in lieu of this favour. They will appreciate this gesture because an eager participant is an anomaly.

You can send WhatsApp messages or emails to the contacts and inform them about the contest in detail. Show them the things they can buy with the prize money, talk about the good performers and the laggards. Be assured that the laggards will be nagged to death once they enter home. The wife will do the job you clearly failed at. This nagging will work like a double-edged sword; the employee will stay at the office more to avoid home, or start improving his performance to please the wife. Either situation will work for you...such a beauty!

Time for an anecdote:

There was once a gentleman who used to report to me. The word 'gentleman' is a euphemism for him, but I am generous that way. He had a little issue with my authority since I was a woman. Not my fault—my gender, but logic was not his strong suit. Whenever I used to hold meetings, he would sit in the front corner of the room, away from the rest of the team, as he felt superior due to experience, not performance. If he chose performance, he would have to sit outside the room, so he was smart that way.

He would often question my authority and experience and I had a hard time with his behaviour, which was bordering on bullying. I tried to reason with him when his performance was much below expectations, and he told me that he didn't like to work with me because I was not 'a loving person.' As a woman, he expected that I would have a 'softer touch' and I would forgo dip in performance vis-à-vis my male counterparts. I told him that for 'love,' he could consider asking his wife, to which he replied that she left him because she thought he was not a loving person.

I suddenly burst out laughing. I couldn't control my softer side. I don't think he took it very well.

I am sharing a sample questionnaire that you may administer to someone you wish to recruit as a team member. This will help you ascertain their usefulness to you.

Answer the following questions truthfully:

1. How many real friends do you have?
2. Do you like to go out to eat or socialize?
3. Is sleeping a necessary activity?
4. Do you like weekends?
5. Do you like doing the same thing every day?
6. If we provide you a place to bathe and sleep, would you consider staying over?
7. If yes, would you get your own toiletries?
8. Do you have a wife?
9. What do you think about work-life balance abolishment?
10. If you do not know MS Office, kindly do not bother returning this piece of paper.

HOW TO MANAGE YOUR BOSS

Suppose you are part of a team, just a cog in the machinery, going about your day being a robot. You will also need to interact with your supervisor and teammates, which can be a challenging and arduous task.

This is a topic that bothers every living working human and it can be a pain managing the giant egos of small men. However, if you note some standard actualities, you can sail through this relationship.

- A boss is a human being, just like you. Remember that.
- A boss loves to be flattered. A boss loves to be loved.
- A boss loves having ample free time.
- A boss likes to go home to his family immediately after official working hours.
- A boss likes his Excels, PowerPoints and reports made

by someone else. You.
- A boss doesn't like it if his boss screws him because of your incompetence.
- A boss blames his team for failure. A boss takes the onus of success.

If you build your relationship keeping the above in mind and all your actions are oriented towards these, I have no reason to doubt the success of your association.

Time for an anecdote: Goldfinger

I had a supervisor who used to come to the office at around 1 p.m. every day. Then he would order cold coffee and a box of sweets. After digesting these, he would take a nap in his cabin and come out at around 5.30 or 6 p.m. Then he would begin asking about the proceeds of the day, collections, sales performance, etc. He would often question me as to why I do not conduct any meeting at around 8.30 or 9 p.m. He would often appreciate my colleague who would conduct such meetings around 11 p.m. He would go home around 12 or 1 a.m. every day and expect everyone to do the same. It was easy for him because he didn't have to report to work at 9.30 a.m. the next morning.

I would tell him that I meet my team at 9.30 a.m. every day, but it was as if this time zone did not exist in his mind. He was very sure that I never conducted any meetings, so I used to take pictures as a record. Once we launched a sales contest and his only contribution to that contest was the below-mentioned SMS:

'Bhaag lo (participate) ya bhaag lo (run away). Kya mein bhaag loonga? (Will I participate?) Keep guessing about

me and decide about yourself. Have a wonderful contest.'

He used to wear a shiny gold ring on his little finger and would often lift and point with it to make a statement. He added meaning to the phrase 'Ugly is back.' He continued in that organization for a few years before he got sacked, for an altogether different reason.

Bottom line: You can't cheat everyone all the time. But you can cheat them long enough and go unnoticed.

Time for a second anecdote:

Many years ago, I had a supervisor who called me at 11:45 p.m. asking me why the sales figures for the day were forty-four instead of forty-six, which was the committed figure. The official working hours were till 6:30 p.m. and the unofficial working hours were till 9 p.m. I could have given logical explanations like unpredictable circumstances or uncontrollable delays, but that would just prolong the call at the ungodly hour. So, I committed to do forty-eight the next day and cover the shortfall. He was immediately satisfied and the call ended.

Bottom line: To deal with a fool, you have to be a fool.

P.S. 46 (committed figure) + 2 (shortfall) = 48, in case you are also a fool.

Time for a third anecdote:

After WhatsApp became popular, a lot of supervisor-subordinate discussions started taking place on this platform, which was both a relief and an annoyance. A relief because you didn't need to hear each other's irritating voice all the time, and annoyance because one could be contacted all the time. There was a situation where my boss was in a dilemma, and both the options available to him were like choosing between the devil and the deep blue sea. So, he wrote to me that he was in a fix, in a 'Catch-42' situation. I was suddenly worried because I didn't know that Catch-22 had an older sibling. I was dying to correct him; the urge was uncontrollable, but I restrained myself from saying something inane. I was just grateful that he didn't type 69.

Bottom line: Don't ever correct your boss, just be grateful.

CHAPTER 4

Emails: Read, Write and Interpret Like a Pro

Emails are proof that you came to office and you worked. An email can present, without reasonable doubt, that you had something to say and that you took the time to raise your finger and press the 'send' button. That is good enough.

When you send many emails, the content doesn't really matter much because most people aren't really going to read through the entire email. But they will remember that an email with your name lands in their inbox many times. It's like an advertisement with your name on it. Whenever you send forwards to customers or vendors, mark a copy to your supervisor. He will appreciate your involvement and 'hard work'. One can be busy sending and receiving emails the entire day, month, year.

HOW TO RESPOND TO EMAILS

There are only three ways:

1. Ask a question;
2. Make an open-ended statement;
3. Never commit to do anything.

The most important question is, 'What can I write when I have nothing to say?' There is the world to write about, the birds and the bees, your neighbour's irritating habits, the pipe that keeps leaking, the hard water deposits in your taps and such things. If this doesn't excite you, then there are other things as mentioned below.

Do you know what a 'quickie' email is? It is an elaborate email write-up about something that happened very briefly, for a few minutes, sometimes even for a few seconds. Quickie emails are convenient, imaginative and extremely satisfying tools much unlike their homonym.

Let's discuss how you can have brief but meaningful experiences that can be substantiated with pictures to create a glorious work of art.

Case 1: *Job fair*
Assume there's a job fair going on in the city. Kindly go there, stand in the middle of the crowd, take a picture and email it to the entire supervisory team stating that you have accumulated many prospects, have slogged through the day and have interviewed a million candidates (could be for anything...sales, recruitment, etc.). The actual time spent here would be close to fifteen minutes. A picture should speak a thousand words.

Case 2: *Road show*
Say you have been asked to do a road show and are expected to shortlist prospective clients. Instal a canopy near a high footfall area, click a lot of pictures of random people from different angles, and that's it. Create a fake list of prospects that has your friends' names and contact numbers. Total time taken: fifteen minutes.

Case 3: *New product launch*
The activity here is to call the entire team to the office in identical t-shirts, with the organization logo. You should be standing on a pedestal, advising your team about something important—that's what the picture should convey. Ask your team members to hail and 'thump their foot' on the ground to exhibit their heartfelt enthusiasm. Take a wonderful picture in fifteen minutes and enjoy the rest of the day.

Case 4: *Team-meeting pictures*
Team-review pictures are crucial to long-term happiness. The frame of the photograph should be such that it includes one individual standing near the white board, with some numbers written on it. The other team members should be seated around the table with laptops and papers strewn around. You should be standing with one hand on your hip and the other pointed at the white board. Total time taken for this exercise: a beautiful five minutes. You can gallantly send an email talking about the motivation instilled in the team members. Please mention the 'charged-up' morale of the team and support the fluff with pictures.

The recipient of this email will believe in his heart that the target has already been achieved and you are solely responsible for it.

Time for an anecdote: To kill a mockingbird

Foot thumping reminds me of an actual incident from my work life. I was in an organization where we were asked, at the start of each day, to gather in a room. We would then thump our foot on the ground and clap vigorously while uttering the words 'Kill! Kill!' very loudly. This was done to instil motivation and awaken a killer instinct. I think it worked...most of us quit. A picture was definitely taken.

Restricted emails

Whenever you want to appear important or the contents of your email to appear important, send them in a restricted format. A restricted format is one in which the recipients need 'certain access rights' to the email. This is an 'improve-my-self-worth' format. It makes the sender and the recipient feel important; use it judiciously.

Motivational emails

You must endeavour to be viewed as a highly motivated, positive individual if you ever want to be successful. The important word here is 'viewed'. A three-minute email with a motivational phrase or a happy picture of a person climbing a symbolic ladder should do the trick. These are the things that make you stand out. People remember such emails that land in their inbox every morning. Again and again and again and yet again.

HOW TO READ AND INTERPRET ABBREVIATIONS IN AN EMAIL

We have already spoken about email-drafting skills. Apart from writing, one also needs to understand how to read. There are things people say in emails but one needs to cultivate the special ability to comprehend the meanings of the words.

Abbreviation	= Meaning	= Actual meaning
EOD	= End of day	= After a few days
ASAP	= As soon as possible	= Never

CC	= Carbon copy	= Boss
FYI	= For your information	= Don't bother
FYA	= For your action	= Don't bother
FWD mail	= Forwarded mail	= Don't even bother opening it
NN2R	= No need to reply	= Fuck off
RSVP	= Repondez s'il vous plait	= Wow! French
Tc and thks	= Take care and thanks	= Asshole

Spend your time on other pleasurable pursuits, not this.

Notes:

Some people take the liberty of addressing others as 'dear'; no name is mentioned after that. For example,

> Dear
> Please send me some irrelevant reports.
> Thanks.....
> xyz

This is nonsense. If they knew the email address, why wouldn't they know the name of the person? Maybe they were acting coy.

And those dots...don't even get me started on the dots......................

A LABYRINTH OF WORDS

In most organizations, the sales teams choose to create an Excel sheet with prospect name, feedback and contact information that is pretty simple to make. See the illustration below.

Sr. No.	Prospect Name	Contact No.	Email	Date of meeting	Next meeting date	Feedback
1	ABC	98233XXX	abc@gmail.com	A date	Another date	Some English words

However, some senior managers and chief executive officers (CEOs) prefer elaborate stories about sales calls with potential clients (prospects). The longer it is, the better. This is done so that they have something to read during their long idle hours. The question is, how to write a long email about something that occurred for a sum total of ten minutes, or worse, never happened?

Please allow me to take you through a sample case study.

Situation: What actually happened

Prospect 1: You met Mr ABC, briefed him about the product and the organization; he seemed uninterested and did not commit anything. An average sales person would understand that this was a lukewarm response and the probability of a sale is negligible.

Prospect 2: You had nowhere to go, so you called a couple of friends and told them you were under pressure and going to type their names in the prospect meeting email and give out their contact details. They obliged. Then you spent about one and a half hours gossiping with them.

What your management wants from you:

Your efficiency is measured by the length of your email and the number of prospects met. So, you try to meet more people (real or virtual) fast, so that you have many stories to tell, even though the possibility of an actual sale happening in any of them is miniscule because there wasn't enough time or effort.

What you write in the email:

Dear sir,
Please find the feedback of my prospect meeting.

Prospect 1:
I met Mr ABC at his office, which was located in the centre of the city and I was a little late for the meeting, but he graciously accommodated me and offered me a drink (of water). I explained to him the vision of our organization and took him through our short-term strategic goals, which he was quite impressed with. I told him about the product benefits and features and how the product fulfils his current requirements. He had certain budget constraints, so he was unable to put a date on the purchase, but he was quite certain that he would buy the product someday. He has been associated with our product in the past, when a close friend of his had purchased it and talked about it very highly. So, he already holds a good opinion of our product, which is the best in terms of quality in the market. My next course of action would be to follow up with him at an opportune time, and push for closure.

Prospect 2:
I met Mr Agrawal at his factory site. He was looking for a technical solution in his current setup where our product could have served the purpose. He was a very congenial person. Even though he

was very busy with his meetings, he gave me a lot of time and was very interested in our product. While he was ready to take a trial of our product for ten days, I told him that we do not offer any such thing. So I was unable to commit to him in this regard. However, I spoke to him for about an hour and a half and we discussed at length about how our product can be the best in the market. While he was convinced about our product, he wanted to move further only after a free trial. My next course of action would be to get him a free trial after discussions with the service delivery team or a distributor.

Regards,
xyz

What your management concludes from this email:

Prospect 1: This guy works hard. A good prospect will be closed soon.

Prospect 2: This guy is good; he spoke for so long. This organization should really offer a free trial. It's a genuine market feedback.

You have been pretty evil in both your emails because you have already built up a case of non-performance due to situations outside your control. In the first case, the prospect had a budget constraint; no money, so no sale. And in the second case, if a free trial doesn't happen, the organization is to blame, and, of course, the prospect is fake, which didn't bother anybody because 'Oh! What a tangled web we weave, when first we practice to deceive.' Shakespeare was so much ahead of his time.

It is easy to create a long email; it is like writing an imaginative story, much like what goes on in children's minds. You just need to observe the things around you and make things up as you run your fingers across the keyboard. And don't worry so much about honesty; it's a virtue that is past its youth.

I have so much respect for people who can create stories out of thin air; it's an art that is not well appreciated. Some people worry unnecessarily about the lack of their English-writing skills.

You must remember that the gist of the story remains the same, i.e., whatever your job was, it will not be successfully completed due to reasons outside of your control and you need to find a person, situation or policy to blame for it.

It's like a low-budget movie, with only three characters.

1) You: obviously in the lead role
2) Person/situation/policy: in the villain's role
3) Performance: as a good friend, who dies midway

The senior management pours in a lot of money producing this movie and then blames the distributor (villain) for not having released the movie in enough screens. This way, the saga continues month after month, but you can be happy you got the hero's role. You got your money; you got the Critics' Choice Award and someone else went bankrupt, thanks to your long emails.

Remember, if a minotaur could be confined in a labyrinth, your boss is cakewalk.

Note: In Greek mythology, the minotaur was a monster that was kept in a labyrinth to contain it. (Just making things easier for you, child.)

CHAPTER 5

Leadership

Leadership is like parenting. Once you have a child, you can claim complete and absolute expertise on the subject. Your child is busy breaking things in the neighbour's house and scattering faecal matter in their garden while you are busy giving advice to new parents on how to raise their offspring. Just because you successfully procreated doesn't mean you know squat about raising a child. The two are very diverse fields; one is a mindless exercise and the other is a mindful one. In the same breath, becoming a leader is only the first step; continuing to be a well-respected one, totally another.

A GOOD LEADER AND SUCH NONSENSE

Some leaders are born with inherent talent that enables them to enjoy situations such as torturing subordinates, talking about meaningless stuff, considering their opinions to be facts and beating around the bush. However, one need not be disillusioned if one is not a natural-born leader. Leaders can be made if they are ready to consume some path-breaking advice such as these below.

Here are the dos and don'ts of being a good leader:

Dos:

- Always hold meetings after official working hours. This proves how busy you are during the day.
- Always call the staff on weekends and holidays.
- The monthly planner should be made many times in a month, preferably every week. Everything should be made only on complicated Excel sheets, with pivot tables, graphs, formulas, frozen panes, etc. This helps to prove that you are smart, even if someone else is making the Excel. (Someone else must always make the Excel.)
- Hold many conference calls; the agenda is not important.
- Send many emails, even if you are just forwarding them. Just mention a one-liner.
- Always look busy in public. Talk loudly on the phone about the performance that you need, even if there is no one on the other side. Scribble on the notepad vigorously, even if you are just drawing flowers or signing your name a million times.
- Always say good things about your boss in public and loudly. Someone will carry the gossip back to him.
- Carry your laptop around the office many times in a day. You should hold it in your left hand and a pen between your lips and a notepad in your right hand. This is a picture of a remarkable leader. So busy!
- Ask for tea many times in a day. This shows that you are very tired but need to keep going. People will think 'this guy must work a lot, he asks for tea so many times.'
- Always look flustered, like you are under a lot of pressure. When people ask you how it's going, always reply with '*Bohot pressure hai, yaar, lagi padi hai*.' (There is a lot of pressure, I am screwed.)'

- If someone comes to you for an approval, always say no the first time. This will prove that you are a hard taskmaster. Who cares if they came to ask you for a loo break?
- Always send delayed emails that land in the inbox at 2 a.m. People will be impressed at your commitment to work. Nobody will question your efficiency.
- Always say that festivals and holidays are a waste of company time.
- Always hang around tea stalls/pan outlets and please, please smoke a cigarette. Real leaders smoke; how else can a man cope with so much pressure? You tell me.
- Always take credit for a job well done. The one who sends the email is perceived as the one having done the job.

Don'ts:

- Don't ever ask for coffee or lemon tea. That is a drink for sissies. You are not one of them.
- Don't say the air conditioning is too cold. I mean, really, true leaders don't let the environment bother them.
- Don't ever say you want to go home early or want to go home. Ever. Leaders sacrifice their lives for their jobs. Work-life balance is for losers. Make up other excuses like you need to meet a vendor or a new distributor, make a sales call or a service call, etc.
- Don't ever say you have good subordinates, because in case of non-performance, you will have to take the blame.
- Don't appreciate your team too much. A light pat on the back is okay; no need to go over the top.
- Don't ever approve leaves of your subordinates. Even on public holidays and festivals. The rule is simple; if they don't work, you will have to.

TASKMASTER IS A SYNONYM FOR SLAVE MASTER

Once you attain a leadership position, it becomes imperative that you stay there without getting canned. This challenging task can seem a little uphill at first but only if you are a simpleton who likes to do a lot of work. For the rest of us, there's a huge opportunity to be a slave master and put every little creature to work.

It's not so easy being a slimeball; it's a lot of mental exercise! You must ensure certain line items, as mentioned below, are achieved at any cost. The rest will just follow.

1. Check the entry and exit timings of all employees reporting to you, because after all, you are nothing but a glorified spy. Use this information to insult them when they are late or leave office early.
2. Call your people at odd hours like 8:30 a.m. or 9:45 p.m. Ask them a few inane questions and take a commitment. Ruin their entire day or night.
3. When you know that an employee has taken a personal day, be sure to call him several times so that it's not a personal day any more.
4. When an employee wishes to take all the leaves he's entitled to, threaten to put him under performance evaluation.
5. If an employee performs well or achieves an impossible task, swoop in to appreciate him and thereby take partial credit for his work. Lay down future expectations, so that it seems like you were in the know of his earlier achievements.
6. When you are working from home, prepare many email drafts on the previous day and send it out at different times on your day off.

7. When an employee gives a commitment on tasks or numbers, be sure to double it or push him to the next impossible level, so it seems like your expectations are very high. Then, after much negotiation, bring it down to the previously committed number, so that your overall target also reduces. This is a great manoeuvre when done in front of your own supervisor; otherwise it's just silly.
8. To bring a little bit of zing in the mundane lives of subordinates, threaten to fire them from time to time. Later on, tell them it was in jest. After all, it's a leader's responsibility to inculcate some dark humour.
9. When you review your subordinates, be sure your boss is present. The entire exercise should be like a circus, you screaming and booing and clapping, and all your team members shivering and wetting their pants. This is exactly how a real leader is, one who is feared.

Time for an anecdote:

Once upon a time, in an organization far, far away, there lived an ogre boss. During reviews, if anyone debated with him or came up with a counterargument, he would turn red and throw the duster, white board markers and other paraphernalia at the employees. He was already the chief operating officer (COO) and was picked up by competition for an even more exorbitant package.

I once had a colleague whose spouse had delivered a baby at the end of day one of the review. He was eager to go home and experience the moment that comes once in a lifetime. His boss denied him that leave of absence and was much appreciated by this ogre boss for his cutthroat attitude.

Bottom line: There is nothing like inappropriate behaviour; only subjugates with high obedience levels.

JUDICIOUS REPRODUCTION

A good leader is supposed to introduce 'truly original ideas' into organizations and teams. But man has existed for a long time, and most of the original ideas are already taken. And frankly, it's a pain to think of something new and unjust to give to an organization where you will float around briefly.

To begin with, a good leader should only perpetuate ideas of no consequence or importance, such as the format of a document, or naming some days 'happy days' (days when an employee overachieves his target). A good leader cannot merely think of achieving a target because that's something you are supposed to do without incentive.

I will come up with some titles that you can repackage for any activity, process or group. The launch of this 'truly original idea' should be done with much pomp to build the tempo around it and to encourage the buy-in of another has-been.

Blue Brigade

This can be used for any team activity during the cricket season in India, so it will seem very topical as well. During Independence Day, the same team can be renamed as 'Tiranga Brigade'. On Christmas, call it 'Santa Is Coming Brigade', and so on.

Good to Great

This title has been used in so many organizations that it cannot be used any more for effect. Nobody calls it 'Crap to Better,' which is the more appropriate term. You can use the term 'Everyday

Excellence'. I just came up with this term in under a minute, and it has a double E. Just think of the logo options you can create; you can be busy for so long a time.

Operation Blue Lagoon

The idea behind this name was that if one wants to increase the sales performance, one needs to look further for customers, make more effort and create a larger prospect database. So, one needs to go into every corner of the lagoon (which is the metaphor for market) and find new and exotic creatures (the metaphor for customers). Somehow, the name 'Operation Blue Lagoon' made people nostalgic about a movie with Brooke Shields in the lead and the activity took an unanticipated diversion. However, you can feel free to rename this 'Operation Blue Sky'; that's also a movie I think, but it doesn't have Brooke Shields in it, so no worries.

Strategic Cell

If there is a bunch of people occupied doing work that has no accountability, and nobody in the organization depends on them for anything, then such people can be placed in a group called 'Strategic Cell'. This group of people has certain traits that are enjoyed by senior management, such as excellent English-writing skills, can make complicated Excel and Word documents, are very good at filling empty words in long presentations and are very good at making graphs and Venn diagrams. Contrary to popular belief, they are not glorified MIS (management information system) coordinators.

In all the above situations, you appear to be doing something meaningful, without it being earth-shattering. And what's in a name? 'A rose by any other name would smell as sweet.' Shakespeare is nodding fervently from the dark side.

A PASCAL OF PRESSURE

In physics, pressure is a scalar quantity; that means it has magnitude, but no direction. In other words, in a volume of gas, pressure is defined everywhere, but its force direction is determined by you.

It is the same in a workplace. You direct the pressure away from yourself to another recipient. If it stays with you, you will not enjoy the feeling; it will make you jittery and a little bit crazy, but as a leader, you will have many recipients who can wilfully absorb your pressure, because that's a subordinate's job. So, be a giver, not a taker.

By the way, pressure is not a new phenomenon. It has always existed in society and you have felt it from the time you were a toddler. Let me refresh your memory with some sentences.

He's one year old and hasn't started walking.

He's six, but his milk teeth have not fallen yet.

When will he put on weight? When will he grow taller?

Why are your grades not better?

Which college will you graduate from?

When will you get a good job?

When will you get married?

When will you have your first child?

When will you have a second child?

When will you die? (Surprisingly, nobody ever asks this, even though it is a logical conclusion in the order of life and the answer is unknown, just like for the rest of the questions.)

The best thing about pressure is that it requires no formal education, no skill; it can be communicated in various languages, it's very easy to create and all it requires is the eruption of a sentence from a mouth.

There is always one person not related to you by blood who is interested in the answers to the above questions. But in your work life, you have the liberty of directing this pressure on to another person who will get married and have the child for you. All you need to do is order, because you are now a leader.

CHAPTER 6

How to Use Emotions Even If You Are Not a Woman?

Please don't get emotional about exhibiting emotions at the workplace. It's really not such a big deal, I know real men don't cry, but I am not asking you to either. In fact, a display of emotions is imperative to distinguish you from the next bot in the cubicle.

There are various kinds of emotions that can be exhibited freely in the workplace, and in ascending order of salience, I present them to you:

▸ Enthusiasm—Always and forever

One must endeavour to constantly exhibit excitement and thrill towards any new job, and very enthusiastically pass them over to the next bot in the cubicle. Some examples of such enthusiastic statements are:

'Sir, I really like performance reviews, they really get me charged up' (a review, not your review), 'Collating data can be very exciting' (by others, of course), 'This time I am going to break all past records of performance' (records have lower and upper limits, don't worry).

▸ Affection (adulation)

I am not asking you to distribute free hugs. But adoration for your supervisor is a must, as mentioned earlier, and so is generous (fake) praise for the rest of the co-workers. Everyone likes a people-pleaser, by definition.

▸▸ Sadness

This emotion has to be exhibited strategically and occasionally, otherwise you may be labelled as a sad sally (a woman). This can be used against you by your supervisor in case of non-performance. If your boss feels you can't achieve your tasks or targets within timelines, you can say, 'Sir, how can you say I can't do it? How can you?' (make your lips quiver, look away, gaze for five minutes, turn)

This sudden exhibition of sadness takes any supervisor by surprise, and they often don't know how to handle it. Hence, the only thing they can feel is sorry for you and guilty of their behaviour. And that, my friend, is just fine.

▸▸ Joy

While joy is an extremely rare commodity at the workplace, one can aim to find it in simple tasks along the way. In case of a very important presentation, fiddle with the projector and make it malfunction. Make an off-site client meeting appointment on a Friday at 3 p.m. and finish your day early (it's not necessary that the client is a real person). Fall very sick on a Monday. Take a pillow, stick your boss's picture on it and punch it hard for a long time. Type your resignation, keep it as a draft and look at it before performance reviews.

▸▸ Exhilaration

This happens when your boss is on leave. The exhibition of this emotion has to be internal. I can understand that you might want to scamper around like a little squirrel, but your face should be deadpan.

- Anger

It is acceptable to exhibit some muted anger towards colleagues and subordinates. That shows that you care about productivity and output. But any anger or resentment towards the boss should be kept bottled up in your heart; let it fester and spread like fungus, let it loose the day you resign.

- Anxiety

Only a confident employee is recruited, so if you are not confident, either you are not an employee, or incorrectly recruited. Both options are dangerous, so being anxious at the workplace is a big no. My advice would be that one should pretend to be stoic and remain indifferent to circumstances that can cause emotional upheavals, such as the time before a review, performance appraisal or a working Saturday. This stoic behaviour will prove with certainty that you are a valuable resource to the organization, even though inside you feel like a meerkat sniffing for danger.

Time for an anecdote:

I had a colleague from senior management with whom I was to make a joint visit to a customer. This senior manager was from out of the country and he was making a routine visit to the India office. He had limited information about Indian roads. As we were driving around town, he showed much apprehension about the overgrown shrubs on the side of the road. He felt that they were a very risky occurrence and could cause road accidents. I told him that we, as drivers, don't let such small challenges ever bother us. We just manoeuvre the car rightly. He told my boss later that I was a very confident person.

Bottom line: Always take foreign visitors for a drive.

Time for a second anecdote:

I had a colleague who was not doing very well on the performance front. She (yes, it was a she, for a change) found herself in the midst of a review and didn't have much to say about her work. Then the topic moved to another subject, where her boss decided she didn't have the expertise or 'wherewithal' to take the unrelated task to fruition. At that moment, she let her eyes fill with tears, ensuring that not a single drop fell out of them. She made her voice quiver, just a bit, and said, 'How can you be sure that I can't do it? I have not done it before, so how can you presume that I won't be able to do it? I was really looking forward to doing this task.'

And then she and her boss went back and forth about it. But with her tears, she persuaded her boss to allow her to keep the unrelated task allotted to her. Conclusively, the boss got a bit ruffled that he made a woman cry (sort of) and he was worried it would escalate into an HR issue. In fact, he was inept at managing the sudden outburst of emotion. So, he noted that he was really happy to have such a passionate employee (though non-performing) in his team and that's the kind of commitment he was looking for. She was a smart cookie, she changed the narrative of the review, she got a new task allotted (a simpler one) so that at the next review she would have something good to show. Subsequently, she got labelled as a 'passionate and committed employee.' Her non-performance was no longer an object of concern.

Bottom line: You can play hardball with tears, but for that, you have to be a woman.

TEAR MANAGEMENT CYCLE

The above anecdote brings me to our next topic—Tear management. Tear management is a cyclical process in which an individual moves from a state of equilibrium to a state of controlled chaos only to return to the steady state. When you master this technique, you can create discomfort for your supervisor at any time while appearing passionate and genuine. And supervisor discomfort is something everyone looks forward to. This process has five steps as explained below:

Equilibrium: Here the employee maintains his composure while listening to the negative feedback received from the supervisor.

Initiation: Certain facial expressions that exhibit angst, displeasure and hurt are slowly introduced.

Filling but not spilling: The eyes fill up to the brim with tears in such a way that no tear falls out of the eyes. This is a key feature of this process and a proper control mechanism needs to be in place. Whatever needs to be communicated to the supervisor has to be done at this stage for maximum effect.

Absorption: The tears have to be reabsorbed into the eyes or evaporated. The use of hands or tissues is to be avoided because then it just becomes a tear fest.

Equilibrium: Return to the state of composure after the said communication and enjoyment of the response of the supervisor.

Tear management can be used under duress, when you find yourself cornered into a situation you cannot get out of. It will create a clear pathway among thorny bushes and you will walk yourself to the other side unscathed, holding a fragrant bouquet in your arms. Your supervisor, on the other hand, will feel as though someone kissed and slapped him at the same time.

Note to self: Apply for a patent for the Tear Management Technique.

Another note to self: Don't be lazy; at least consider applying for a trademark.

A third note to self: You are so smart.

Time for an anecdote:

I had an employee reporting to me who was stationed at another location. His hometown was the head office location and he used to commute to his allotted location. I had received a feedback from the channel partners that he hadn't visited the location or their office for many days. When I tried to cross-verify this from the employee, he used this tear management technique on me. His eyes filled with tears, his voice quivered and he told me he would never do such a thing. He said that he was always present at the said location, but since the last few days he had been going back home early because his father was very ill. In spite of being a woman, I saw tears in a man's eyes and I fell for it. Of course, I found out later that it was a lie. He cheated me with his tears and taught me that tears are powerful but need not be truthful.

Bottom line: A teary-eyed man is a rare phenomenon; enjoy it, but don't get swayed by it.

THE HAMSTER'S WHEEL AND SUNDAY EVENING BLUES

A lot of people keep hamsters as pets in a transparent cage and give it a wheel for exercise. The hamster is dumb enough to feel it is going places, even though it is in the same place. Sometimes, middle managers are not as dumb and hence get afflicted by a virus called 'existential crisis' from time to time. They begin to question the purpose of their presence and the futility of their job roles. The only way to protect yourself from this disease is to vaccinate yourself with a drug called denial. Everyone has some of it in reserve; all you need to do is summon it.

How does denial feel like?

Denial is like falling in love with a serial womanizer. You know it is going to end badly, but you hope and pray it will go away. You believe you have the power and skill to change his womanizing ways, you believe the strength of your love will keep him in your arms forever and he will never desire to be in a new pair of arms again. You market yourself hard, you advertise, you give trade discounts and consumer freebies, but the product (you) falls flat on its face. You were in the wrong market segment in the first place, but denial kept you in a dreamy haze.

Similarly, in the workplace, denial is the belief that your supervisor will reduce your targets if you stop achieving them. Denial is also the belief that things will be better in another organization when your own baggage remains unchanged. However, denial can be a great escape at the workplace and you need it because you love money.

Anthropologists who research how Eskimos adapt to the Tundra must also consider studying denial as a survival technique.

Sunday evening blues

Most people live their life during weekends; at least they try to. When you pack in so much punch in two days, there is bound to be a withdrawal from ecstasy. You have to be a little more measured. Do not detach yourself totally. You can always depend on your boss for some help. A phone call here and there or a couple of emails will keep you in the zone. You will never be completely out of it, so there will be no blues.

CHAPTER 7

The Art of Delivering Presentations

POWERPOINT—I LOVE YOU

PowerPoint is a revolutionary invention and there isn't a manager worth his mettle who will disagree with me. So revolutionary it is, in fact, that even school-going children are being forced to learn it. It seems in the future all important communication of information will have to happen through this platform for it to be legitimate. And once we have successfully indoctrinated this technical art form into a generation of people, some smart-arse will come up with an upgraded version.

A complicated PowerPoint presentation can make even a fool look good. Ask a smart colleague to help you make a presentation.

The slides must contain:

- Graphs
- Tables
- Coloured templates
- Complicated Venn diagrams
- A flowchart

If you have these, you are already winning. The kind of data that has been used to make these is absolutely irrelevant. Nobody will question the logic of these graphs and diagrams for fear of appearing stupid. A few pictures of the tasks completed (refer to 'Quickie emails' in Chapter 4) would be like a glass of cold water after a spicy meal.

The last slide should be the target for the month. This should be an absolutely preposterous, unachievable number. Never achieved in the past and never achievable in the future. When you reach this slide, be sure to shout out these numbers with the utmost confidence and say, '*Hojaayega, boss, thok denge numbers.*' (It will happen, boss, we will achieve the numbers.) If your boss doesn't smile, and love you, I will courier the proceeds of this book to you.

On a side note, if you can link an Excel sheet to your presentation, nothing like it. It's just magical when you open a PowerPoint slide, click on a link and an Excel spread opens. It's like a new level within a level of Angry Birds.

How to present a presentation:

- Keep your hand on your hips to make yourself appear bigger than you are.
- Pace around the room like a caged tiger.
- Whenever you commit something, shout loudly and confidently. Don't ever worry about achieving it. It's the confidence of commitment that matters, not the delivery.
- When you present your shortcomings, just don't present them.
- Use the word 'Boss', 'Chief' and 'Sir' many times.
- If questioned on how you plan to achieve your targets, just smile and say '*Hojaayega.*' (It will happen someday long after you have left the realms of the earth.)
- If your boss says, 'You have never achieved these numbers in the past, how do you plan to do it this month?' Just say,

'This month it will happen.' Then smile. Your mysterious smile will make your boss feel that you have some trick up your sleeve and that maybe you will perform this month.

LONG PRESENTATIONS: A STUDY OF PROS AND CONS

A long presentation is a facade and it's often very successful in misleading the audience with data that don't necessarily prove the achievement of the presenter. But there is so much information that people get confused and don't realize that this data was presented by someone else at some other time. When you have nothing to show for yourself is the time you should consider making a long presentation.

Pros:

- The fact that it is long is an achievement in itself, because you had so much material to begin with.
- Halfway through the presentation people get bored. They stop paying attention, so any big mistake will be overlooked.
- After the first nine slides, the patience of the audience will be wearing thin, so you can rush through the presentation citing lack of time.

Cons:

- Typing so much and pasting graphs is a time-consuming and often boring exercise, which you may like to avoid.
- You could spend this time sleeping, chatting or watching something nice on Netflix.
- Finding the material to make such a presentation is often the trickiest job; if you had an assistant, he could help, but you don't.

HOW TO CRITIQUE A PRESENTATION IN A PUBLIC FORUM

This is a tough one. You will not only have to speak rudely, but you will have to show that you were actually interested in the presentation. And you will need to remember a few things about the presentation to speak about it. But I can give you simple pointers that can make your job easy. Utter these sentences at the beginning or during the presentation and see the magic unfold.

- 'What kind of fonts are these? You should have used something better.'

This can be used for any presentation, irrespective of the content. And you can sleep through it. You need not bother about the response to this comment either. Fonts are a matter of personal choice. Some people **like this** and some people *like that*.

- 'You keep saying the same thing every month. Nothing changes.'

This statement says more about you than the presenter. It says that you pay attention to his presentation every other month. That means a lot. A lot!

- 'Why can't you be more enthusiastic about your presentation?'

This always puts the presenter on the back foot. Because he thinks, 'I wasn't enthusiastic? Why did he think so? Is it my shirt? I just washed it yesterday.'

The presenter loses focus and invariably fumbles, and that makes you look good. It also makes you right. Bullseye.

- 'I am unable to understand what you are saying.' Or, 'I am unable to comprehend your point of view.'

The important thing to remember while uttering this statement is that you must appear dead serious, otherwise people will think you are a fool. Be very serious, crimp your forehead, put your hand on your chin and nod your head sideways.

▶▶ 'Can we move to the next slide please? I got your point.'

This line conveys two things: i) You 'get points' very fast so you must be smart; ii) You still want to move to the next slide.

▶▶ 'Why don't you give me a ballpark figure?'

You used the word 'ballpark'. Most people don't even know what that means. Only a smart person uses words that others don't understand. Smile and stay motionless. You are a winner.

▶▶ 'All this is okay, but what about the numbers?'

Only an absolute idiot would respond to this question with 'What numbers? What the hell are you talking about?' There is always some kind of data in every presentation; it can't be all fluff. Well, it can be, but let's not lose focus here. When you use the word 'numbers', you invariably appear as an analytical, number-crunching smart-arse. 'Nuff said.'

CHAPTER 8

What Are Organizations Built On?

As you move higher in the organizational hierarchy, you will notice that your love for formats increases. I don't see any reason to resist this change; it is only a natural professional evolution. It need not be unnecessarily misinterpreted as a reduction in real work or intelligence. Rather, think of it as an artistic standardization that is beyond the scope of your control. It's easier to surrender to a culture that is going to infect you anyway, and you must aspire to find your mojo in conformity. I say this because conformity, compliance and adherence are the three most loved words in any organization. If you want to stay, then you too must love.

FORMATS, FONTS AND EXCEL

Formats

I am a little overwhelmed with emotion as I type these words. If there is something I have learnt in so many years of servitude, it is this: making wonderful, meaningless, complicated spreadsheets, graphs and project documents. I can make even the simplest of things look extremely tricky. I can make a simple one-line strategy into a mammoth convoluted document.

The basic idea of a graph is to make numbers understandable. It is to give some meaning to numbers. But in an organization, the more obtuse a graph is, the better is its acceptability. It cannot be a bar graph alone; it's too simple. Obviously, it has a domain, an axis and a range. I think I lost you there.

Let me make it simple. Whenever you create a graph, it should have a couple of things. A bar graph should have a line running through it or a line graph should have multiple lines. (It should look like an electrocardiography [ECG].)

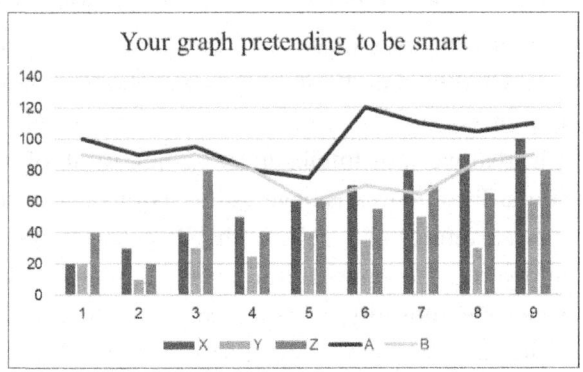

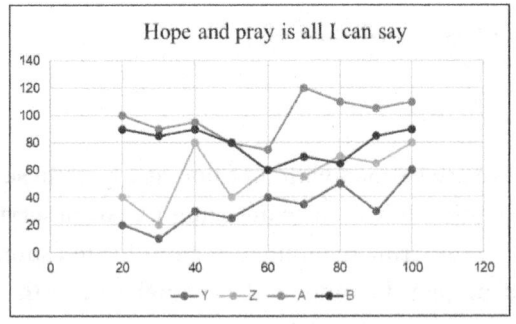

Eventually you should create graphs that look like a weather forecast.

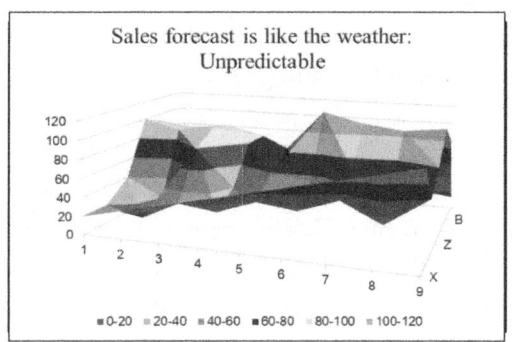

If you are on a psychedelic trip, you can use this one.

Now I am just playing with you, but you know the gist. The idea is to create a picture that looks too complicated to question. Questioning such a graph or its complexity would invite speculation about your intelligence. This is not data interpretation, it's data disintegration.

Fonts

Some supervisors are fanatic about font type and their size, I wonder why. Microsoft Office has provided a range of options to suit every personality, and don't we always want diversity in the workplace? But I feel a militant choice of fonts proves a leader's power, makes it seem like he is calling the shots, even though he's a machine—just like you. So, once you are in a leadership position, it's always good to be vehement about your font choices; it never goes wrong; it's a stand that's widely admired, even though it's so absurdly stupid.

In every organization, there is a uniform choice of fonts that percolates every document; it's a part of the organizational style and behaviour, and it supposedly brings uniformity of thought. Unless someone researches this and has a decent sample size to prove it, it's just hearsay. But hearsay is great, and well-constructed statements in English are always believable.

Try this:

Uniformity of fonts brings an alignment in thought and process, hence should be considered to be of utmost importance before the construction of any process document.

This statement can be true or false—nobody knows, because it has not been statistically validated with a decent sample. But see how authentic it sounds...and don't you like the business-like font?

Microsoft Excel

Microsoft Excel is an excellent way of proving that you are intelligent and mathematically skilled. You will need to make some effort to learn the goddamn software, which is a pain, I understand. Because it's fine to not be a graduate for a position, but it's not at all fine to not know MS Excel. MS Excel knowledge is the minimum criteria to be considered for any position; it's a prerequisite, just like MS Word. Nobody cares if you don't know basic spellings, because the cure for idiocy is the gift from Bill Gates. I will give you some tips that can make any simple Excel look as if it has been created by a very competent person.

First and foremost, remove all the grey-coloured gridlines. Make the Excel look like a Word document. Why, you ask me. The answer is quite simple: a face without wrinkles looks younger, and you may consider looking at it longer because it is pleasant to do so. Gridlines are unwanted lines and easy to remove at the click of a button. In real life, one can never erase wrinkles, which is again just as unimportant an activity. Don't quote Botox because it is frightfully expensive and mostly you cannot afford it. And even with Botox, the number of people looking at your face will be quite inconsequential.

Anyway, coming back to the point, make a smart Excel rather than a regular one because that's what competent people do.

Whatever size of font you have in mind, choose one size smaller. If you are a man, I want to tell you that smaller is better in this particular situation.

>> Smaller fonts look intelligent because you have to pay attention and try harder to read them. See, this is an intelligent-looking font and seems like it holds some great unmissable secret just because it's smaller. Try putting an asterisk* like this

one somewhere; that also works. People go out of their way looking for *. I have never understood why.

- The heading fonts should be white in colour with a grey background, and no other colours should be used in the Excel sheet, except red or blue, to highlight certain data points. Because data is supposed to look grey—just like the performance results.
- Always add comments in some of the cells to make it look like a well-thought-out endeavour.
- Left or right or centre align the data—whatever floats your boat.

This is, of course, the bare minimum; I could bore you with more, but why should I?

Look, a regular Excel sheet is a pudgy man in an untucked half-sleeve shirt worn sloppily over ill-fitting pants. He is in open-toed sandals and scratching his beard with dirty fingernails. I know that you know I didn't mean 'beard'. A smart Excel sheet, on the other hand, is a fine young man in a nicely cut suit with a smile on his chiseled face. Ask yourself, whom would you stare at more?

I could have given the same analogy with a woman, but the problem is that no matter what she wears, she's stared at, so I just cut the idea loose.

ENGLISH—YOUR FIG LEAF

If you are a remnant of India's colonial past, you will definitely agree with me on the importance of the English language in the social hierarchy. I don't know what is so special about this language, but the moment it exits a person's mouth, they are viewed as erudite, and belonging to the upper class. It's no different at the workplace. English is the key to a world of dreams. Big words, jargon and sentences that mean nothing, these are the things that differentiate you from the rest of the morons.

Let me guide you with a list of sentences that would help present you as a smart, knowledgeable resource to the organization. These sentences mean nothing and carry no accountability, so don't worry.

▶▶ We must be able to see the big picture.

Huh? How can someone reply negatively to this statement? You have to say, 'Yes, that's true' or 'Sure, we do.' It seems like you are a far-sighted individual who has the capability to foresee the future.

▶▶ I had used this strategy with much success in my previous organization. I got a lot of recognition for it. We can do a 'pilot run' here.

The response to this statement is invariably: 'This guy seems good. He just used the word "pilot run".'

▶▶ Market research data states that 'blah, blah is true.'

Nobody questions such data. Listeners just feel 'Wow! He knows about market research.' If someone chooses to verify the source, just name a fake source like Nielsen-Smith or the Draconian-Green survey. If the name sounds foreign, it should work.

▶▶ Competition is offering better service to the customers than us.

Any statement can be made about 'better service'. You will be surprised how poorly informed your co-workers are about the so-called competition.

▶▶ This is a very exciting plan. This is a very exciting project. This is very exciting!

People will feel, 'what an enterprising guy', or 'I wish I could be so excited about this shit'.

>> This is the most important month of the year.

This is the mission statement for all sales personnel. You can never go wrong with this statement. In fact, you will be viewed as a serious, target-oriented 'Employee of the Year'. It is one of my all-time favourite sentences.

>> We must achieve our targets this month *at any cost.*

This always evokes a positive response. Nobody is going to say, 'Please don't, spare us this time.' People always feel 'At least he wants to.'

>> Yes, it's very difficult, but possible.

No supervisor wants to hear the words 'not possible'. So, this is a nice way to say no.

>> I will not let you down this month, 'sir'.

Hahahahahahahah. Ha!

>> Let's discuss this offline.

What this means is 'let's not discuss this at all'. This is a beautiful way of avoiding confrontation. I personally love people who use this sentence. They are so chicken.

>> I want this relationship to be meaningful to both of us.

Ok. Sure. But is this a marriage? In a way, it is. It is a marriage of the minds. You can use this with your subordinates, vendors or anyone reporting to you, directly or indirectly. It is a condescending statement of power.

>> Let's do a sales blitz. Let's do a market-mapping activity. Let's go for a market visit. I am on a market visit.

All this means is, 'Let's get out of the office and go wherever we feel like'. In this context, 'market' can mean various things, like a 'doctor's office', 'home', 'shopping mall', 'your kid's school', 'movie theatre' or 'café'. Technically, all these are kinds of markets. However, the speakers of this sentence are always viewed as hard-working individuals, putting in lots of effort.

▶▶ Let's look at this holistically.

What does one do when asked to do this? Absolutely nothing! No one, I mean no one, can object to this sentence, it sounds so holy.

▶▶ Let's get our priorities realigned.

The answer to this statement is always a 'Yes, we should'. Because nobody dare say, 'What is the meaning of realigned?'

▶▶ Let my LIPs meet your TIPs. LIP = Lateral implementation plan. TIP = Tactical implementation plan.

Are you feeling embarrassed? Don't be. These are real things in the real world. But you've got to be a man to say it.

▶▶ Let's collate the data and do a digestive analysis.

All you are saying is that just look at the picture and tell me a story. Just remember to throw in words like cost curves, pro forma financial statements and annual reports. You will probably become the CEO.

▶▶ Let me touch base with _____.

Fill in the blank with any word, and it will work.

You can say the marketing team, clients, vendors or my inner self. It's fail-safe.

▶▶ Let's brainstorm and see.

What is a brainstorm anyway? They are just random thoughts that pop up in your mind from time to time. In the real world, you are going to be loved for saying this.

▶▶ I just want to put this train on the tracks and I want to do it myself.

Nobody is going to be searching for the metaphorical train. People will say, 'He really wants to put himself out there', 'He's so eager to participate' or 'He's so enthusiastic about getting results'.

These are the 'normal' responses people will have.

The probability of rising up the hierarchy of any organization is directly proportional to your command of the English language.

So, if you've had your formal education in the vernacular medium, then my sympathies are with you. But the good part is that most people use only a handful of sentences like the ones mentioned above, so you can just memorize them.

In any organization—as in real life—English is your pride, it's your weapon and it's your fig leaf.

LOVE NOTES FROM SENIOR MANAGEMENT

Sometimes senior managers like to show off, and at other times, they just don't know what to do. So, they spend their time writing notes to the other managers who are lower down in the hierarchy. These notes are like love letters, except that there is no love in them. The language is ornate, there are many analogies, there are tangential references and much expectation. After sending such a note, they either ask for a read receipt or they eagerly come to your desk and ask gleefully, 'Did you read what I sent?' The response they expect is one of absolute adulation and astonishment for their ability to express well-articulated ideas. They are quite delusional about the depth of the ideas camouflaged in the flowery language. In other words, the ideas have no depth. Most people are unable to move past the first few lines because the language is difficult to comprehend and it fails at its primary job, which is clear and easy communication.

Sample love note:

Folks:

As we step into the luminous new financial year, I am duty-bound to share my feelings on the acquisition process and deliverables.

I concur with the fact that it may be imprudent to be troglodytes in such a dynamic business milieu. However, to consider the organizational tools as your principalities is to do a disservice not only to the company but also to yourself. In your endeavour to do so, you make your rendezvous with success ephemeral. The rapacity to accomplish the allocated goals should not override you such that you engage in many inexactitudes that may be detrimental to the prospective clients or may persuade a churn of the existing clients. If you choose unscrupulous methodologies, it may be a Faustian bargain in the long run.

You must be steered by the ethical guidelines set forth by the organization to keep you on the straight and narrow. Ultimately, it will be what sets you apart from the rest of the herd.

Regards,

Your guiding spirit

P.S. *James Joyce is turning in his grave.*

If such a note lands in your inbox, or worse, you get a hard copy, run fast and long.

CHAPTER 9

Meetings: An Evergreen Tool

People hold meetings to pass time and build pressure. I am all for passing time. I mean, you landed in the office and you are being offered a salary; the least you can do is huddle together in a room and talk. But new managers sometimes don't know what to do in a meeting. They feel, if something can be communicated over a phone call, why waste everyone's time in a meeting? New managers are modest people; they can be forgiven for their simple living and high thinking.

To be successful in the workplace, appearing to have many meetings to attend is very important. Meetings keep you busy and are an excellent substitute to work.

AGENDA OF A MEETING

Below are a few programmes that need no preparation, thinking or action on your part, and you can consider using them often.

Performance review

This can be done two or three times in a month. If you have nothing to do and have a team of people reporting to you, this is the best thing to do. You have no contribution here. You just need to get angry, feign frustration at non-performance and pressurize them to perform, while offering no support. Keep saying things like, 'I am answerable to the top management for your dismal performance' or 'I need you guys to go all out; do what you have to, but get the job done' or 'I can't do your job for you'. After this, you can go back to your cubicle and watch the new show on Netflix.

Planning

Planning is a method where people sit together and make a plan to do nothing. How this nothing will be achieved is done on a pre-ordained format provided by the management. The targets are predetermined, so not much work there, and there's not much you can do every other month to manage the competition either. Hence, you sit around a table, treat yourself to biscuits and tea, and grumble why the administration team cannot offer some other hot snack on an important day such as this. You know 'a friend' in whose office they have installed cold coffee and iced tea vending machines, and discuss how these things really improve the work environment. This way, a couple of hours pass and your salary is justified.

Agenda-less meetings

There are occasions when people from different departments convene to discuss the 'support required' from each other. This is called an agenda-less meeting. Whoever is seniormost in authority acts as the compere in the meeting and people just keep talking over each other. This is a collective decision to get together to fool the management where a mass exodus from the cubicle to the conference room is required, which can happen only if some spicy snacks and creamy biscuits are in the offing.

Time for an anecdote:

I had a supervisor who used to conduct meetings every week to discuss target vs. achievement, and asked employees for revised lower targets all the time. After the meeting, he would call again after two days, asking about the revised commitment. This way, time used to pass every month, and he built a reputation of being a tough boss, which worked in his favour. It's another story that targets were never met.

Bottom line: Foolhardiness builds reputation.

MAKE YOUR PRESENCE FELT

You can start by never being the first person to speak at the meeting. People have a lot of energy at the start of a meeting, so don't ever choose to speak then. Once everybody is exhausted and wants tea and biscuits, that is the time you need to deftly put your points across. Nobody has the willpower to pay attention, and your presence will be noted but not criticized.

Meetings are what make an organization worth working for. The more the meetings, the less the actual work. So, why would you choose otherwise?

If you want to make your meeting appear important, and want more people to attend it, then you must create a hype around it. First, book the conference room by sending an email to the admin guy. Mark a copy to everyone who's invited. Send an email about the agenda in 'English'. Do mark a copy to your boss. In the agenda, all participants should be allotted some task for which they need to provide feedback. This is so that you can watch, do nothing and just keep criticizing. Blatant criticism will ensure that your presence is felt. Your boss will also feel you work a lot.

Confirm with every email recipient about the attendance and preparation. If someone is absent but has sent feedback on the task beforehand, you can mention 'in absentia' in the minutes of the meeting. That word always looks so smart. Walk hurriedly across the corridors the next day to appear busy and thoughtful. Always carry a piece of paper or a file in your hand when you do so. That makes it all very believable.

WHAT TO SPEAK IN A MEETING?

This is a pain-in-the-arse thing. But this book is a beacon of light in such trying times. I have had people talk for hours about the same thing. You can keep your mouth moving, people can hear a lot of different words, and time passes.

Irrespective of the agenda of the meeting, you can begin by talking about your experiences in the professional world. Talk about your years of experience and the ways in which you tackled various hardships. Talking about one's achievement in retrospect gives the latitude to be pompous, and not completely truthful, which is a nice thing.

Here are a few examples:

- 'My boss had given me a target that was never achieved before. So I zipped up my pants, took out my cigarette, went to the nearest tea stall and started thinking, how do I do this? And just by the sheer determination of my thoughts, I did it.' (Remember, this was all in the previous organization.)
- 'You know, when times were tough, I used to always do

things differently.' (This may sound clichéd and lame, but no one dares to question it.) Lateral thinking is crucial in such situations.

▸▸ Then talk for five to seven minutes on the agenda—whatever that is. Mostly, it would be dipping performance. Because performance is always dipping.
▸▸ Then talk about the areas of improvement, the support needed for the same. Ensure that the support you are asking for can never be given. So, later on when you fail, you can always blame the lack of support.
▸▸ Try to make a joke. Everyone likes a funny guy. Just safeguard yourself against being the joke.

Time for an anecdote:

As a management trainee during my early years, I was a part of a group that was assigned mini projects. These projects would be reviewed randomly by a mentor who had no social life. These meetings used to be painful and slow, much like your career. I had a colleague who at the time suffered from a case of incomplete evacuation (popularly known as constipation) rather regularly. He would carry a small tiffin box filled with raisins, dates, seeds and other such items that apparently helped with this malaise. One Friday evening, as most of us were preparing to leave early with sweet dreams about the weekend, our mentor decided to call us for an impromptu meeting. Most of us were really bummed with this development as we assembled in the conference room. Suddenly, the air was rank with a peculiar, pungent and noxious smell. After waiting a while for the air to clear and holding our breath multiple times, the meeting was adjourned in search of a dead rat. We were eternally grateful to our colleague for the airborne gift as we enjoyed our weekend as planned. This non-traditional approach to problem-solving was lateral thinking on jet fuel and a salvation for new office-goers.

QUARTERLY OFF-SITE MEETINGS: PRESENTATIONS, BOOZE AND VULGAR DANCING

Every once in a while, organizations give employees a chance to unwind, let themselves loose and be free, if only metaphorically. Off-site team meetings and presentations are a good way to push for performance in an informal and friendly environment, especially when the evening ends with some alcohol and dancing.

A lot of individuals dislike this situation because they can't let themselves loose in public, and find it uncomfortable to watch others do the same. But in order to be popular, you have to enjoy these company-sponsored picnics. I understand that you need to sit through some godawful presentations and commit to deliver on your commitments. But that's a small price to pay to be viewed as a team player. At the end of the day, there's going to be free booze and you can dance your pelvis away to the raunchiest of songs. There are some key points to be noted here:

- Your after-hours performance is more important than what you did during the entire day.
- Your presentation doesn't matter as long as you have committed to deliver something crazy.
- You need to trot around the rest of the evening as if you have already achieved your target.
- Tell people that you love your job, and this time the team and you are really charged up.

Soon the time will come when alcohol will appear like rainfall on parched land.

How to behave when alcohol is as close as a mother's hug? There are three distinct ways:

- Jump on the drinks like a thirsty dimwit. Most of your superiors will appreciate your zest, and you will seem like a supercharged person.
- Drink a lot but be subtle about it. You will be well appreciated for your ability to 'hold your drink', which probably means you are a very strong person.
- Drink a lot and lose your self-respect completely. Believe me, this doesn't work badly for you. People will talk about you the next day and how crazy you were. You will be the talk of the party for your foolish exhibition and no one will ever consider you a poor performer. Because they will not remember anything else about you after this night.

If you are a teetotaller, then there are issues, my friend. It's a sad and difficult day for you. Your choices will be a burden on you. It's a grim day to begin with, and you will be labelled a loser. If you can and will dance, then it can save the day for you. Some enlightened souls view teetotallers as lacking testicular fortitude and as going against the will of nature. The only way to show that you are a merciless go-getter willing to embrace your raw and natural self is to dance shamelessly.

If you are a woman who chooses to drink at a work gathering, you may be susceptible to a harsh judgement of morality. If you are a woman who does not drink, then why be in a man's job, they will say. It's like one of those dreams where you walk in naked into a packed room, awkward and not really fun.

THE FINE ART OF DANCING AT OFFICIAL PARTIES

Most people can't dance and are rhythm-deficient. This is something no one readily admits. There are many who do not like to jiggle their lards in public. Then there are most that do.

It's the sad truth, but if you wish to be viewed as a team player and a go-getter, dancing is a must. You must be able to fling your arms in the air, bob your head sideways and jump around like a two-year-old. You must be able to sway your pelvis vigorously when the music hits a high note. You should be able to hold the 'Elvis pose' at the end of each song.

Dancing after drinking alcohol is like sailing on a yacht in the south of France. Feels great, but not everybody can afford it. When the day is over and everyone retires to the room in a semi-conscious state, they will remember all those with whom they had fun. If you are not a part of their collective memory, you will pay for it. On the ride back home the next day, people with relive those exciting moments of booze spilling and cheap dance moves. They will all look at you and call you names if you choose to be a prude. Most importantly, your boss will say, 'You should learn to be a team player', and that will be a blot on your appraisal. Any moral or religious stands about alcohol will make people shut up, only to get back at you at an opportune time.

My advice: Drink like a maniac and dance like a loser and you will be a winner.

CHAPTER 10

Politics: When It's Fun for Everyone

Organizational development books define the positive face of politics as a balanced pursuit of self-interest, a relative absence of tactics of fighting and an absence of hidden agendas. This definition is right—in exactly the opposite sense. To make it clear and easy, let me introduce you to some necessary conditions. Please note the mantra of office politics as below:

- Every organization has the same kind of people.
- Everyone gossips.
- All human beings love flattery.
- Everyone is devoted to someone.
- An office spouse can be a reality.

Let us now focus on the kind of participants who partake in office politics, namely, everyone.

PARTICIPANT CATEGORIES

Identification of participant subtypes makes it easy to stereotype them and predict behaviour, which, in turn, makes your case stronger.

The Snake

A snake is a person who is insecure about his position in the organization. He lacks the courage to face up to challenges, situations and people. He has limited knowledge about his job. He will appear super friendly and will immediately assign a relationship status to your casual acquaintance. For e.g., statements like 'You are like my brother or sister or father or mother.' No fool says wife or lover. He will camouflage his lack of skills with skilful sycophancy. Be aware of the snake because a snake slithers and a snake bites. A snake has fangs it does not show.

An office snake is a stealthy predator and will harm you when you least expect it. A snake is afraid of people with knowledge, ability and courage. So, he is definitely not afraid of you.

The Dog

As the name suggests, it is a servant of its master. This person will do anything for his master, the boss. No job is menial for him. Laundry, bill payment, car wash, grocery errands, a dog can and will do anything for its master. Dog-Man sits late in office doing boss's work. Dog-Man picks master from home. Dog-Man delivers movie tickets.

Dog-Man does everything, apart from his official duties. Dog-Man always covers his boss's tracks.

Tackle Dog-Man as you would tackle a real dog. Feed him, walk him, talk to him, give him a little rub behind the ears. And chain him up when he goes bad.

The Pussy

Don't let the name confuse you. A pussy cat is a wild thing. It purrs and moves around noiselessly but will scratch your eyeballs out. I want to say that such people generally appear more effeminate than they should be. But I won't say such a thing. Pussies are silent people who can be ferociously selfish. They will not bother you if you are not in their way.

The Horse

Hard-working, diligent, loyal, smart and good-looking. What do you do with such a person? I am at a loss! If such a person happens to be your boss, you either start working or quit. If such a person happens to be your colleague, you either start working or quit. If such a person happens to be your subordinate, then prop your legs up on a sofa, open a can of beer and say cheers!

The Lizard

A lizard is the master of all data. The data is on the tip of his tongue and all the other tips of his body. He has performance data, competition data, market analysis data, new product data and market research data. He has the data of your past failures. A lizard eats small insects and flies to survive. You are the small insect. Remember that.

A WEB OF GOSSIP

If the stock market is based on speculation and people make an informed judgement built on that, I see no reason why gossip should be treated otherwise.

I read somewhere, 'Gossip is news running ahead in a red satin dress.' I feel that's an accurate description. Gossip keeps you ahead, because it is information that can turn out to be true or false. In case it is true, you win, and in case it is false, you don't lose. The thing about gossip, though, is one should always have the gossip; one should never be the gossip.

You must stay abreast of the happenings around you, and if you wish to be included in a higher social class within your office, you can begin by perpetuating some gossip. People don't differentiate between fact and fiction as long as it is about someone else. Gossip can be very effectively used to make friends at the office, ostracize a person who bothers you or just to vent off some steam. Even those who seem aloof or unaffected by office gossip love to hear it because gossip is like junk food—unhealthy but attractive.

FLATTERY—MY FAVOURITE SIN

Flattery is defined as insincere praise, used to further one's self-interest. But most people accept it as genuine praise due to issues of their own self-worth, which is a great thing. Flattery fills up the gap in performance, helps you make friends, and people like to have conversations with those that think well of them. Those who have certain inhibitions about flattery and find it untruthful, I want to emphasize that it's only a matter of perspective.

When you say, 'I think you look so beautiful,' the attributes of beauty, the benchmark against which this judgement has been made, whether the person looks better than their previous self or whether it is the inner beauty that is being referred to, are never questioned. This statement is accepted without prejudice because it is open to interpretation.

When you say, 'I think you are a very smart person, sir,' the same rules apply. And one need not always refer to the dictionary to utter words of praise.

When you say, 'I want to be like you, sir,' you are not referring to any particular trait. You may want to be as tall as the person, or have a similar haircut or buy the same brand of toothpaste; it could be anything. It's wonderful to hear some subtle flattery because it sounds very sincere and truthful. Some examples are:

>> 'I find your way of doing things very efficient.' (say it with a straight face)

Since it is subject to interpretation, it's not a lie, and no superlative terms have been used, so it sounds nice and believable.

>> 'Multitasking is not as easy for me as it is for you.'

Any person who is not a woman can utter this statement and it will be true. And when you use it for a man, he will feel very pleasant about it because it will be the exact opposite of what his wife believes.

>> 'You are effortlessly handsome.'

A good thing that comes without effort is a welcome phenomenon.

>> 'I know you are overburdened with responsibilities.'

This is flattery because you have made an assumption that the person has a lot of work that can be termed as 'responsibilities.'

These one-liners can be used for supervisors and co-workers, or anyone who is useful to you. Use them often and see your stock soar.

OFFICE SPOUSE

People always misconstrue this word and start to attribute moral values, cultural idiosyncrasies and other such useless variables to this simple relationship. An office or work spouse is a person of the opposite sex with whom you share a close bond, someone who can work as your eyes and ears, and their loyalty to you is assured. This is mostly a platonic relationship—similar to most marriages—so nothing sacrilegious here. There is so much to vent in a work environment, and having a loyal and discreet-sounding board can do wonders for your mental health. Often when both of you are workless, you may just sit together with a laptop and pretend to be busy—an excellent relationship to cultivate.

POLITICALLY CORRECT BEHAVIOUR

I believe in giving it to you straight up. I am not going to serve an undercooked and poorly spiced meal on a beautiful porcelain plate with cheap wine and call it gourmet. In the workplace, if you want to be well-accepted and charter a smooth path to the top, there are some hard truths to follow:

- Always appreciate your boss in public. Appreciate those qualities that he doesn't have.
- Always bad-mouth your boss's boss in his presence.
- Always be extra nice to everybody during the first introduction.
- Always snitch on your colleagues to your boss in a discreet manner.
- Always reach office five minutes before the official time and send an email then. Remember: An email proves that you worked, and it marks your presence.
- Always call your boss at odd hours and ask inane questions to prove that you are always on the job.
- Be everyone's friend.
- Give hollow smiles to everyone; ask them if they need any help.
- Share your tea, lunch, pen and paper with all and sundry.
- Don't accept accountability too easily; always try to beat around the bush.
- Make friends by doing favours—just like in prison. You can always ask for it back.
- Wear your boss on your head like a crown and make him feel special each time, every time.

Try it today!

CHAPTER 11

Women in the Workplace

This is such a tired subject and has been talked about ad nauseam at different forums.

Seriously, what a bore!

Some evolutionary mechanism decided that women were going to be the better-looking human. Just look around you and you will notice that the average woman attracts more eyeballs than the average man. This anecdotal evidence only proves that women are more attractive than men. What else could explain the constant staring at public places?

When the distracting good looks of the female employee are clubbed with efficiency, multitasking abilities and resilience, they make for formidable and jealousy-inducing co-workers.

They push the existing benchmarks higher, and that can be very frustrating for the other employees. When a beautiful and well-spoken intelligent woman makes a presentation, and you are next in line, it really dampens your spirit. Tell me, why do we need a spirit dampener in the workplace? For some reason, if there is an efficient woman colleague in the office, all the men start getting compared to her with statements such as:

'If she can do it, why can't you?'

'She's a woman and you are a man, but still she is doing better.'

'How long are your target achievements going to be lower than hers?'

'You also start wearing a skirt from tomorrow.'

Some people take the liberty of saying 'bangles', 'blouse' or 'bindi' instead of 'skirt', but it means the same thing, so don't get confused. In short, an efficient woman's presence can create a state of dichotomy in the workplace and it cannot be for the best, can it?

There are some qualities that are unjustly used for women, such as multitasking abilities, empathy and the ability to handle problems. Instead, the qualities that should be noted are the ability to tolerate injustice, play second fiddle without a fight and accept the superiority of the man (as it should be—I like men). So, it is only right that they should be confined in their traditional roles for the smooth functioning of society. There are girls from privileged families who are well educated, with degrees from foreign colleges, and then they come back to marry rich men and become social butterflies. The education and class were to enable the sourcing of a wealthy spouse. This is an example of following a traditional role in spite of the freedom that an excellent education offers you.

Bottom line: Harass men by being wives, not co-workers.

WHAT TO DO WITH A FEMALE EMPLOYEE IN SALES?

The argument:

Women have no place in sales. They want to go home early because they are afraid of the dark. They have husbands and children to look after, so they spend less time in the office. They have premenstrual syndrome (PMS), so they are pissed off for a week every month. They go on maternity leave and you can't even fire them. Sales is a man's job!

The counterargument:

Women tactfully get what they want, which is another word for 'persuasion'; they are excellent at nagging, which is another word for 'follow-up'; they can find the right person to get the job done, which is also called 'being resourceful'; they can talk for hours together with anyone, which makes them 'personable'; they know how to convert a 'no' into a 'yes', which can be termed as 'objection handling' and they invented emotional blackmail, which can be loosely termed as 'closure'.

Additionally, evolution made them pleasant-looking, which gives them a higher probability of a patient hearing by a prospective customer. Tell me, why should it be a man's job?

Time for an anecdote:

I was told by my boss that I had been retained in the sales team in spite of being a woman because he believed that I was different and I could achieve my targets. When I asked him what he meant when he said I was different, he said that I was not like most women. I wanted to do 'something' with my life and I had a drive. He said that his supervisor didn't believe in my abilities, but he had taken a chance on me, so I must prove him right. Prove him right by being just like the rest of the women or by being like a man? I was confused. So, I waited and I waited and eventually he found an exciting new job.

By the way, his wife did do 'something' extraordinary; she continued to live with him.

And his mother showed quite the drive to birth him.

MATERNITY LEAVE: THE CURSE OF THE FREE WORLD

What do you do when a woman employee reporting to you declares she's pregnant?

When one is accustomed to a luxurious life and a highly competitive sperm tries to mess with it, it's annoying, to say the least. You can work harder or begin to work (in some cases), but that takes effort, and it's not something you want to do. That's what an impending maternity announcement is; you can no longer explicitly pester that employee to do your work.

People ask, 'Why come to office if you want to have babies?' They say that once pregnant, you must retire from work and embrace the role nature envisioned for you.

Because being a mother is enough, you shouldn't pursue much else, should you?

Some organizations commendably go out of their way to ensure that they help women stay in these natural roles; by providing no flexible work timings, no crèche facility and no job roles for women wanting to rejoin work after a postpartum sabbatical. So, if you want to be rid of this employee, then the system will work in your favour. But better to exhibit some concern for this employee before cracking the whip to avoid looking like a sadist.

You can pretend to care about the employee's health by asking her if she's regularly going for her doctor's appointments. This way you know when she is out of the office.

Tell her that if she doesn't feel well, she can take time off. You will be able to predict her postpartum work ethics from the amount of complaining she does when pregnant. Predictions need not be based on any scientific forecasting methodology for them to be accepted as true. The strength of your belief is directly proportional to it becoming a fact.

Build up a case of non-performance and keep it handy. The moment she returns from her maternity leave, bombard her with this.

Keep uttering statements such as:

'I gave you as much maternity leave as you requested.' (Doesn't matter if you were just adhering to the company policy.)

'Do you get, enough time to work?' (Nobody will retort, 'Twice the amount you get thumb twiddler,' so relax.)

'I supported you when you were pregnant.'

'I think I have given you enough time to perform.'

'Nine months is enough time to perform.'

Anyway, best to be rid of this employee, or if that's too challenging a task for you, delegate her to some inane job role, like stapling papers.

(On a side note, there was a supervisor who actually made these kinds of statements. I gave him a reply, which I cannot share here because that would make this book unsuitable for family reading. But it was the most pleasant feeling I had in a long time.)

MULTITASKING: IT'S NOT A WOMAN'S BIRTHRIGHT

I bring this subject up right after the maternity leave for a reason. After having kids, most women are unable to do justice to their careers. They have to manage their home and kids while paying attention to their job or career. It's impossible for anyone to multitask like this. That is why I say, 'Get rid of this employee.' So much cannot be accomplished in twenty-four hours.

Some idiots would argue that having kids increases your multitasking ability. But then, why argue with idiots? Some fools even go to the extent of saying that kids increase your patience and tolerance levels which can, in turn, help manage your boss. There might be a bit of truth in that, but who cares!

In the real world, multitasking would mean the following:

1. Making a PowerPoint presentation for your boss and yourself.
2. Finishing your grocery pickup while screwing your team over a conference call.
3. Enjoying your quarterly holiday while pretending to be sick.
4. Taking your spouse house-hunting while sending emails on the phone.
5. Having a spicy snack on the street corner pretending to be on a sales call.
6. Attending a wedding party while sending emails on one phone and talking on the other.
7. Keeping your phone number diverted on the same number so that others constantly get a busy tone. How can you enjoy a movie during official working hours otherwise?
8. Keeping your phone out of coverage area while pretending to be on a sales call in a remote area when you are taking a nap.
9. Playing Solitaire on your laptop and all the while nodding your head during a meeting, pretending to take notes. (It's difficult to play Angry Birds because the excitement would be palpable.)
10. Having a tea party at a local street shop with your colleagues and telling your boss you are working on a new idea.
11. Asking a colleague to collate data for your monthly reports and convincing him to make an Excel spreadsheet, so

that you may enjoy the time taking your girlfriend for a drive while telling your wife you are in a meeting. (This actually happened.)
12. Managing your alternative career/business while claiming business-meeting expenses and conveyance expenses from your current organization. This is the epitome of multitasking. If you reach this level, then I bow down to you.
13. Motivating a competent colleague to quit his job while pretending to be his friend so as to erase the threat to your career.
14. Pretending to be someone's confidant and then spilling his beans over to your boss and then lending him your shoulder to cry on.

Multitasking can be so much fun and reminiscent of a soap opera. It can brighten an otherwise dull existence in a cubicle, and it makes your resume look nice!

HOW TO BE A CLANDESTINE PREDATOR

The problem with most women is that they don't understand romance or friendly jokes. It's like they don't have a sense of humour. If it's so funny to a man, it's the same for a woman; it has to be, since we are equal. Most people get caught because they engage in overtly romantic gestures; they want to make a big show of it and they want to do it multiple times with different women. That's not how this works. That is a sure-shot way to get caught and be labelled a predator.

First things first, establish a respectable relationship by addressing the female colleague as a sister or treat her just like a mother. You can also choose to address her as 'Madam' if you are the rustic sort or 'Ma'am' if you are the polished sort and 'MAAaam' if you are Irish.

You can say things like, 'Your haircut makes you look so hot, you remind me of my sister.' The woman will be flummoxed because you said 'hot' and 'sister' together. She has to smile and say thank you.

You may say, 'My mother is a gorgeous-looking woman, just like you.'

You can say things like, 'Generally, I don't appreciate anyone, but I can't resist doing it in your case.' This makes it seem like you are not the appreciating type, but she must be a really worthy candidate.

Ask work-related questions by leaning over her shoulder, just grazing her body slightly and looking into her computer. Don't look into her eyes; just enjoy the feeling and let it look like an honest mistake.

When you exchange papers or files or pens, touch her fingers slightly and it should be okay. Such contacts can't be avoided.

When you are in a crowded lift, try to protect her with your body as a shield from others, whether she needs your protection or not. You were only trying to be like a brother.

If a woman claims she's unwell, check her temperature by placing your palm on her forehead or neck. This is obviously important so that any kind of first aid can be provided.

Pat the female employee on the head if she does something right, in a patronizing manner, and let it linger. At least you got to touch her hair and her skull.

When a woman colleague does something cute or funny, laugh out loud and give an impromptu side hug or slap her shoulder as if it was something that happened on the spur of the moment. Later on, you can say, 'Sorry, yaar, but that was too funny' and go back to laughing.

What to do if you can only use your eyes?

There are going to be dull days when no contact is possible because every day cannot be a Funday. But there are ways in which you can use your eyes the way a vulture does; it can look at its prey from afar.

You can check out a woman's wrist, neck, chest area or even the fingers; what's not to like in fingers? If she's clad in a demure sari, there's still the back and the waist you can look at, or even the arms. I know that you also have arms, but just give it a shot. Even a woman's silhouette can be enjoyed.

There are no laws against this; nobody can point a finger at you and say you did something inappropriate. It is wrong to call this lecherous behaviour because all you did was look. If one has eyes, one sees.

All of my examples are subtle and practical ways of being a clandestine predator, and that's just an exaggeration for a friendly person. The world doesn't understand, and that's okay.

HOW TO BE A (HEALTHY) MAN

Where else am I going to talk about this subject apart from this chapter? I am one of those people who catch a cold in India when someone sneezes in Iceland. Out of 10,000 people who eat an ice candy from a street-side vendor, I am the statistic who gets jaundice. So, if you happen to be one of those creatures who have been bestowed with robust health, thanks to your stupid genes, then I have no love for you. The point I am trying to make is that a healthy and strong ox is a welcome phenomenon because everyone likes to own an ox that can toil for hours doing the same mundane task with great enthusiasm each day, every day. An ox that can be whipped from time to time but only toils harder with each whip is an excellent saleable commodity.

I know you are wondering what all this has to do with being a man. Being a man and being a healthy man are two different things. A healthy man is one who is perceived as being strong, aggressive and unperturbed by the environment. This is how you can prove you are better than a woman.

You can project this image by saying things like, 'I never feel cold; I never wear a sweater, it's hardly cold,' even if the air conditioning is on full blast (at freezing temperatures). For some reason, the ability to withstand cold is considered to be a very masculine trait in our country. It may be because it's so hot most of the time.

You can say things like, 'The last time I had a fever was in 1947 or 1999.' (Quote any year you fondly remember.)

When the day has been long and many sales calls have been attended, yet the target has not been met, say things like, 'The night is young, I am so fresh; we can easily pull through.'

'Let's knock on doors and get some business.' This statement is a show of strength because you are not tired even after a long day of non-performance. For some reason, bosses always believe there is some very cooperative customer who will buy the product and hand over a cheque in the middle of the night; they are so desperate to believe anything when targets are not met.

If you remember, in mathematics, theorems used to have necessary and sufficient conditions to be proved right.

E.g.: A necessary and sufficient condition for a quadrilateral to be a square is that it is both a rhombus and a rectangle.

Statement: I am a healthy man because I can do both (i) and (ii).

i) Necessary condition: A man eats a lot all the time.

ii) Sufficient condition: A man can go without food all the time.

(It is the contradictory nature of these statements that makes the theorem all the more exciting.)

Solution: Say things like 'I eat ten eggs for breakfast' or 'I can eat twenty rotis on a regular day.' This does not prove you are a glutton. It just proves that you are a strong man with a large appetite. On other occasions, say that you can go without food for long hours, you can manage your hunger very easily. When you are working, you don't think about food at all; you get so engrossed in your work that biological needs don't bother you.

The whole point of this exercise is to convey what makes your masculinity so special. Because being a man is not enough, because being on the top of the food chain is not enough, you have to make a show of it.

I say with great pride that I learnt this from a man, and I accept it with humility.

THE JOY OF SITTING LATE IN THE OFFICE

I know in my heart that most of us would love to run home just when the school bell rings. But that's not how it works.

Sitting late is an important way to communicate to the boss and the rest of the staff that you are a hard worker.

This is one aspect where you can be much better than a female colleague. She would definitely have problems sitting late, especially with all these fake predatory behaviour stories. She may have kids, which makes it all the better for you. You are not the primary caregiver, so you can stay back in the office for as long as you like.

Nobody would consider you inefficient for not being able

to finish your work in the eight and a half hours allotted during the day. Most people, especially your boss, would consider your resilience and hard work an asset. He is making this judgement only by looking at you sit late. Isn't that an easy way to earn brownie points? You might grumble that you wish to spend time with your family. But do that during the day, no? What is the problem? The moment the clock strikes 7 p.m., you should prop yourself at your desk, look into the computer screen and start typing.

An easy way to communicate that you work hard is to be visible in the office after work hours and sending emails at that time. If you leave office on time, then you give others the wrong impression. People think, 'What is this? Doesn't he have any work? Why is he leaving so early? He has to be a poor performer.' You get labelled as a person who leaves office early and conclusively are not a very hard-working person. If you say that you have no work and hence you leave, then that's even worse. When you have no work, that is the time you need to stay late at the office the most.

So, take my advice on this. Do whatever you want with your life, but in the office, always sit late.

Time for an anecdote:

In some organization, Wednesday was 'family day' and people would get emails from the HR, stating, 'Today is family day; finish your work early and reach home by 8:30 p.m.' I guess the person sending the email had really understood the power of sitting late.

CHAPTER 12

Performance Appraisal: Judgement Day

It's just another day, folks, in your eventless life. It's nothing life-altering, like a promotion or a raise. That was sarcasm, in case you are confused. It took you a while to figure that out... no wonder you are here, my friend.

Anyway, if you have chosen to go through this drudgery you call work, it is advisable that you do it well. Appraisal is that time of the year when you will need to wear your thinking cap to prove on paper why you should really be paid. You will need to prove why they can't hire someone else in your place. You will need to prove why you should continue, even though the numbers mean the contrary. You will need to prove that you are an unfulfilled promise that is yet to realize its true potential.

This uphill task will be achieved by none other than your appraiser, your boss. He is the one who will help you achieve your true greatness, because he's a taskmaster who is known for his perseverance. He is the one who can guide you to the right path. He is an able leader and a great man. Be sure to let him know of your strong feelings towards him. Everyone likes a devotee. Everyone likes to domesticate a devotee. Throwing you out will not be good for his ego. Your job is safe.

APPRAISAL FORMATS

Appraisal forms can be daunting for the uninitiated. There are so many questions about yourself and the work that you do. And most people have nothing much to say most of the time. But this is a good time to put your English language writing skills to good use. You have to be imaginative. You need to brag about yourself unabashedly.

Remember one rule: Always evaluate yourself with the highest rating. Eventually you are going to be pulled down. But there is only so much further down that they can take you.

I am going to present some sample formats that you can sensibly reproduce whenever the need may arise. And, like Voltaire said, 'Originality is nothing but judicious imitation.' So, feel free to copy and paste.

Subjective evaluation sheet

These may concern questions regarding your intangible skills. They are popularly called personal effectiveness rating. These are the skills that are judged on the basis of your relationship with your supervisor. There is no objective data to support this. So, this can go both ways. Let me share with you some sample questions and answers. I am sure you will find them insightful.

1. *How would you rate your communication skills? Cite an example to support your statement.*

Sir, I have excellent communication skills. Everyone says that I can speak very well. I have a good sense of humour. E.g., People laugh a lot when I speak. When I send emails, people are very satisfied reading them because no one ever feels the need to reply. You can check my inbox.

2. *Are you a team player? Support your answer with examples.*

How can anyone say that I am not? Whenever I go out for lunch with my colleagues, I never pay the bill. Someone always agrees to foot my bill because I come up with many excuses to give everyone in the team a chance. That shows my concern for the team and asserts the fact that I am a team player.

3. *Cite an example of your leadership abilities.*

(This space has been intentionally left blank.)

4. *How would you rate your integrity and ethics?*

I would rate them very highly. Whenever any vendor has tried to give me gifts during Diwali, I have never accepted them. When they persuade me a lot, I tell them to send those home and never to the office, since it is not allowed. I never forward company emails to any person apart from friends and family.

5. *How would you rate your adherence to timelines?*

I have good adherence to timelines. I sit very late in the office, till 10 p.m., or sometimes even till 12 p.m. I am committed to my work; that's why people say, you work so hard outside the office the entire day and then you work in the office at night. You can check my timings from the system-generated log sheet. There is a swipe every day at 9:30 a.m. whether I am there or not. That is my commitment level.

6. *Have you taken any new initiatives in your current job role?*

I take initiative every day when I decide to come to the office. Whenever my boss shouts at me, I take the initiative to keep quiet and bear it. My request for a raise has been refused three times and I take the initiative to continue in this organization.

7. *Cite some examples where you have exhibited high efficiency levels.*

Whenever anyone has tried to allot a new task to me, I have very promptly found a suitable excuse to pass it over. In fact, my efficiency levels are so high that I have not been considered for any new task in a long time. You can check the last five minutes of the meeting emails and you will notice that the number of tasks in which I have ownership is zero.

Objective evaluation sheet

This rating system is based purely on numbers, and evaluation is done against the target allotted for the employee. Several organizations take pride in the objectivity of their appraisal systems. They have complicated system-generated appraisal formats with the targets pre-loaded for every employee, and many people, primarily from the information technology (IT) department, work hard to keep it functional.

However, no matter how robust the system is, there are always humans who know how to beat it. And your supervisor is one of those humans who wields the power to bring some personal prejudice into this robust system. One must remember that targets are directly proportional to your negotiating ability. Please remember to keep your boss's boss happy as well, because he would be the reviewer on your appraisal. So, in totality, you may need to polish two pairs of shoes.

There is a 'comments' section at the end of such appraisal sheets. This space has to be filled with the most vague and unusually rich English vocabulary. It reflects that you might be an erudite person with a worldview that is complex and difficult to understand by, say, an otherwise simple person. Your supervisor may not like being viewed as a 'simple' person. He is nothing but an intelligent, educated man of the world. Hence, you might get some points for your English; you always do.

There is a grade curve, popularly known as the 'bell curve', into which the entire employee strength will need to fit in. So, a little bit of flattery and lots of boss service will ensure that you are pushed a little higher than you deserve on this curve.

Time for an anecdote:

It so happened that my supervisor was having some difficulty filling up his appraisal form. There were too many questions, and he had spent half a day typing a single line. After being pensive for long, he called me to his desk and asked me to give him a few pointers. I told him to give me some time on his laptop and I filled up his entire appraisal form with elegant language. He was astonished to see the task completed so beautifully in so short a time, when all he had expected were only a few pointers. I told him it was easy because he had done so much work. I was pushed higher than expected on the bell curve in that appraisal cycle.

Bottom line: Perform at the right time.

Personal effectiveness

Some organizations call subjective evaluations personal effectiveness rating as well. Renaming things is an organizational mantra. Here, the expectation is that the employee must mention intangible non-measurable traits about himself and substantiate the same with evidence.

There will be some big words thrown at you and you will need to explain if you did something to follow those values. 'Value' is just another name for 'word'.

You can always say that you adhered to a value even if you didn't, because the opposite of 'absolute truth' is also 'absolute truth'.

How do I know this?

(Absolute truth in philosophy is defined as inflexible reality. That means it is a fixed and unalterable fact.)

Danish physicist, a specialist in quantum mechanics and Nobel prize winner, Niels Bohr, said that there are 'Two sorts of truth: profound truths recognized by the fact that the opposite is also a profound truth, in contrast to trivialities where opposites are obviously absurd.'

Unsourced variant: 'The opposite of a correct statement is a false statement. But the opposite of a profound truth may well be another profound truth.'

There...now you believe me? In philosophy, many realities exist, and that should work for your moral compass.

Coming back to the task at hand, let me introduce you to some of those values and also teach you what kind of sentences express them accurately. Match the following:

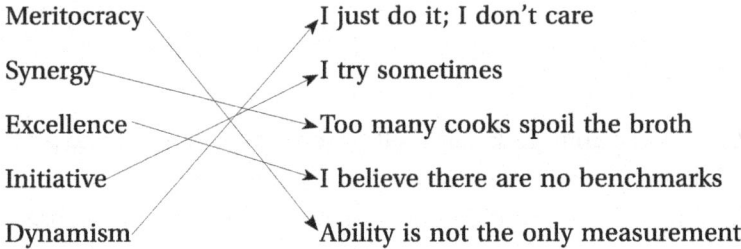

See, once you know what a value stands for, it's easier to attribute it to yourself.

CHAPTER 13

Temporary Redemption

Sometimes, you may choose to discard your workplace for another one because it seems like a better opportunity or the commute is shorter or just because your sanity demands it. This period, between the past and future workplace is a happy, albeit a transient one.

Ichi-go-ichi-e is a Japanese cultural concept translated as 'for this time only', 'once in a lifetime or 'one time, one meeting'. The idea behind this concept is to appreciate the beauty of fleeting moments despite their transitory nature. This appreciation will build the strength to deal with the insanity at the future workplace.

However, the road to transient nirvana is a bumpy one.

THE URGE

As you sit at your desk, engulfed by the oppressing walls of your office, sipping milky tea with lots of sugar and inhaling the stale air from the air conditioner, your mind wanders. You loosen the noose around your neck by tugging at the tie. You feel like throwing that ugly laptop bag out of the window.

You imagine that you are in a small English town, sitting

al fresco on elegant oak wood furniture with a glass of wine. It is a beautiful summer evening and the temperature is a pleasant 22 degrees. The air is sublime with a very low air quality index (AQI) and it fills your lungs with vigour. You are in designer clothing, looking dapper. The man-purse lay beside you and you glance at your watch to see that time has stood still.

As you awaken from your stupor, you look around and think aloud, 'What the hell am I doing? What is this life?' Suddenly, a familiar urge creeps in. You have tried to control this urge, this monster, but it corners you. You are not able to shake off this feeling and it gets the better of you. You open your laptop with the determination of a man possessed.

You log on to Naukri.com and update your resume. Your time here is done.

RESIGNATION: FREEDOM AT MIDNIGHT

A beautiful day.
A day when you can take it no more.
A day you will relive many times in your life.
A day that can happen anytime you wish.
A day of freedom and new hope.

When do you resign?

This is an important question. You resign only when you have a new job in hand; otherwise who is going to pay for your mundane existence? Maybe you are an aristocrat or married up. Maybe you believe in simple living and high thinking. But the rest of them desperately need money to buy food. When you feel you cannot take it any more and need to get the hell out of the claustrophobic atmosphere, start looking for a new job. Try not to feel like this very often. Your threshold should be at least a year. One needs to develop resistance to this virus that has a very high rate of mutation.

Do you tell people where you are going?

Sometimes it's better to answer a question with another question. Are you a person who appreciates a prank call to your future employers about your competency and work ethics? If you are not such a large-hearted person, then it's best to avoid the urge to blurt out the name of this future workplace. You could cook up a story of the excellent new position you have been offered. Talk about the high percentage of raise you have been able to negotiate. Why bother with the truth? Truth is boring, and it has no ability to make people jealous.

The true meaning of a notice period

Imagine yourself in flowing white robes, running through tulip fields. You can feel the breeze on your skin, the leaves on your fingertips and the gush of freedom running through your veins. That's exactly what a notice period feels like—it's heaven. And since it's so ephemeral and infrequent, you must endeavour to make the most of it.

Scamper around like you have nothing left to lose, come and leave as you wish. This is like being in a happy dream. Ensure to submit all your expenses and claims to the administration department so that you don't miss receiving a single paisa from this godforsaken place.

Eat, travel and relax because history will only repeat itself.

Epilogue

Nice to see you come this far, dear reader. I hope this instructive book adds some humour to your otherwise dull day. The thoughts I passed on in this book occurred to me in the ample idle time that I had in my various meandering workplaces. Many years ago, when I began my career, I was quickly struck by the ineffectuality of my workplace existence. I wrote something at that time and I will leave your august company with those lines.

> There was once a girl who got bored of her job,
> Repetition and incompetence made her a blob;
> Slow people and dimwits made her cry,
> All she wanted was to die;
> Dumb policies and stupid subordinates,
> And to add to that she had to coordinate;
> Targets that can never be reached,
> And a salary that made her screech;
> Help! Help! she gave a cry,
> No one to hear except a fly;
> Maybe I can become a movie star,
> Pretend to be a priest at the altar;
> I shall pray and predict the stocks,
> And get screwed in the confession box;
> I want Fame and Money,

Want it in a jiffy, honey;
Want to be loved and admired,
Be the one everybody desired;
Sitting on the chair I write songs,
When targets are the ones that I should long;
Maybe this job is just a farce,
The poet in me is about to barf.

Made in the USA
Monee, IL
03 May 2026